BOSTON and BEYOND

BOSTON
and
BEYOND

Discovering Cities,
Harbors, and
Country Charms

SHEILA MOESCHEN

Globe
Pequot
Essex, Connecticut

Globe Pequot

An imprint of Globe Pequot, the trade division of
The Rowman & Littlefield Publishing Group, Inc.
4501 Forbes Blvd., Ste. 200
Lanham, MD 20706
www.rowman.com

Distributed by NATIONAL BOOK NETWORK

British Library Cataloguing in Publication Information available

Library of Congress Cataloging-in-Publication Data
Names: Moeschen, Sheila C., author.
Title: Boston and beyond : discovering cities, harbors, and country charms
  / Sheila Moeschen.
Description: Essex, Connecticut : Globe Pequot, [2024] | Includes index. |
  Summary: "A guide to dozens of places in the Boston region that offer
  hidden charm, fun, novel discoveries, and original experiences. The
  locations featured in this book are within striking distance of Boston,
  allowing for convenient day trips and enjoyable excursions to charming
  locales"— Provided by publisher.
Identifiers: LCCN 2023056290 (print) | LCCN 2023056291 (ebook) | ISBN
  9781493075836 (paper : alk. paper) | ISBN 9781493075843 (electronic)
Subjects: LCSH: Massachusetts—Guidebooks.
Classification: LCC F62.3 .M64 2024 (print) | LCC F62.3 (ebook) | DDC
  917.4404—dc23/eng/20231220
LC record available at https://lccn.loc.gov/2023056290
LC ebook record available at https://lccn.loc.gov/2023056291

For Todd J.
A treasured friend, a gifted artist,
my wanderlust chum.

And for Kate, Christina, and Mary
who find beauty everywhere and in everyone.

Contents

Introduction   9

STROLL DOWN SIDE STREETS: Pretty Cities   13

    Boston, MA   14

    Salem, MA   72

    Lowell, MA   88

CATCH SOME OCEAN VIEWS: Seacoast Towns   103

    Rockport, MA   104

    Gloucester, MA   108

    Plum Island and Newburyport, MA   127

    Marblehead, MA   134

    Portsmouth, NH   140

DISCOVER BEAUTY ON EVERY BACKROAD: Country Charms   153

    Concord, MA   154

    Cambridge and Watertown, MA   167

    North Andover, MA   173

    Harvard, MA   175

    Lincoln, MA   177

TAKE THE SCENIC ROUTE: Unique Destinations   181

    Ipswich, MA   182

    Bolton, MA   188

    Lee, NH   190

    Concord, MA   192

    Philipston, MA   196

Afterword   201

Acknowledgments   202

Index   203

About the Author   208

Introduction

New England is overrun with an embarrassment of historical, natural, and unexpected urban riches. Tranquil seacoast towns teach a masterclass in the art of slowing down. Thriving cities keep their historical legacies alive and well on every block. Lovely natural locales just outside city limits are overrun with I-pulled-over-for-this beauty and awe in every season. All you have to do is take a little time to look around and see it. As a proud, lifelong New Englander, I'm thrilled to be your traveling companion through this area of the country that means a lot to me and contains countless unique scenes, interesting finds, and memory-making experiences.

Boston and Beyond is, in part, a valentine to the place I've always called home, even during periods of my life when I've lived elsewhere. Yes, we complain about the seasons—all nine of them it seems—and we don't make driving in some of our cities very fun or logical. But underneath our salty, New England exterior lies a lot of love for and pride in the gifts this part of the country brings. New Englanders embrace the annual rhythms in our towns and natural settings. We celebrate calendar shifts in big and small ways, which means there is always something new to see no matter how many times you might visit any given place. A trip to Salem, Massachusetts, in the spooky orange heart of October is a whole different experience than it is in the long, lazy golden hours of July. Head to wooded trails in the winter to soak up the profound stillness that will come alive with birdsong and animal chatter in the matter of a few months. A drab, unremarkable city block suddenly astonishes with brownstone window boxes that run riot with spring flowers in gelato-inspired hues of pink, lavender, and yellow. No matter where you plant your feet or find yourself in the course of the calendar, the sights and atmosphere of just about anywhere in New England invite you to slow down, stow your phone for a few minutes, and enjoy connecting with your surroundings. That's my New England: both timeless and ever changing with beauty everywhere hiding in plain sight.

At its heart, *Boston and Beyond* encourages you to nourish your curiosity and entertain a slightly different approach to taking an excursion. When visiting a place, anyone can handily compile an itinerary of "things to do": activities for every taste and inclination. What about creating a list of "things to discover"?

New England comes bearing some pretty serious street cred. By that I mean we take our share of historical bragging rights. For instance, the American Revolution started here (ever heard of it?). And we claim plenty of show-stopping sights—our wild seacoast, iconic urban architecture, the entire autumn season that sets off foliage fireworks everywhere from mountain valleys to swamps to our own backyards. In between there is subtle charm, elements that create a kind of everyday wonder adding to and enriching New England's appeal. Here, I wanted to call out these aspects to not only celebrate New England's treasure trove of beauty, but to empower readers to light on whatever brings them joy and uplift right in their own hometowns and favorite regional spots.

With this in mind, I've organized this book in such a way as to invite readers to look closer, to notice the environment and the aspects of a place that they might ordinarily overlook. In that respect, this book joins a growing offering of other works about the intrinsic value of reclaiming our time and attention in a distracted world. It's my hope that this will inspire readers to think about how to scratch beneath the surface of a place to uncover something new and experience delightful encounters that resonate long after leaving.

As I said, there are endless things to see and do all over New England. This book is far from exhaustive. After all, half the fun of visiting any place is peeking around new corners to see what lies ahead. Instead, I've curated a travel sampler platter of sorts to give readers a taste of what the region has to offer, ordered to keep travel time relatively short to maximize time spent getting to know and enjoying these various places. Boston is the beating heart of the Bay State, and it's from here that I've dropped a pin to anchor this journey. Boston not only has an exciting array of things to take in, but it's an easy hub for travel both within and beyond its limits. Each additional destination explored in the book falls a little over an hour or less from Boston. Whether you have a handful of hours or a full day, you'll still find something interesting and enjoyable to experience; after all, it only takes a moment to make a memory that lasts a lifetime.

I've chosen a mixture of locales that often fall under the radar when people think about making a trip to New England, but offer untapped reserves of beauty, history, culture, and atmosphere. The opportunity to highlight places of interest that don't always get their time in the spotlight, but have something special to offer, is partly what drew me to this project. By inviting readers into destinations that are more densely woven into the fabric of New England, I hope to empower a "love it like a local" attitude that fosters an appreciation for the urban and natural diversity of the region. As you roam the pages of this book, you'll meet grand summer estates belonging to the capitalist royalty of America's Gilded Age; you'll walk in the footsteps of those fighting for American independence; you'll drift through waves of New England sunflowers; and you'll get a glimpse of life and labor in the textile mills at the epicenter of the American Industrial Revolution.

Photography is a form of visual storytelling and what better place to showcase this than New England with its varied architecture, diverse geography, and distinct regional flare. The images I've selected throughout each section evoke the character of a location, offering readers a sense of the essence, charm, natural wonder, and enjoyment of a particular spot. I make some light suggestions on how to move through some of these destinations and what to look for, but readers should feel empowered to delve deeper and head off in their own directions. As such, I also hope *Boston and Beyond* sparks readers' creativity for how they might see, perceive, and engage with any geographical locale. What happens when you stop to take in a piece of public art or hike an unfamiliar trail? What might you find attending an annual, local festival? I encourage readers to take what they might learn or discover here and carry it forward in a renewed appreciation for and curiosity about the world in their own backyards, down their own city blocks, or in their own town centers.

Lastly, a very brief note on some terminology. To respect the history of Native American ancestry in the United States, I use the term "resettled" when referring to the New England cities and other areas established by European colonizers on Native American land.

Enjoy uncovering and getting to know some of the most original, intriguing, and scenic cities and one-of-a-kind locales that make New England endlessly wonder-full.

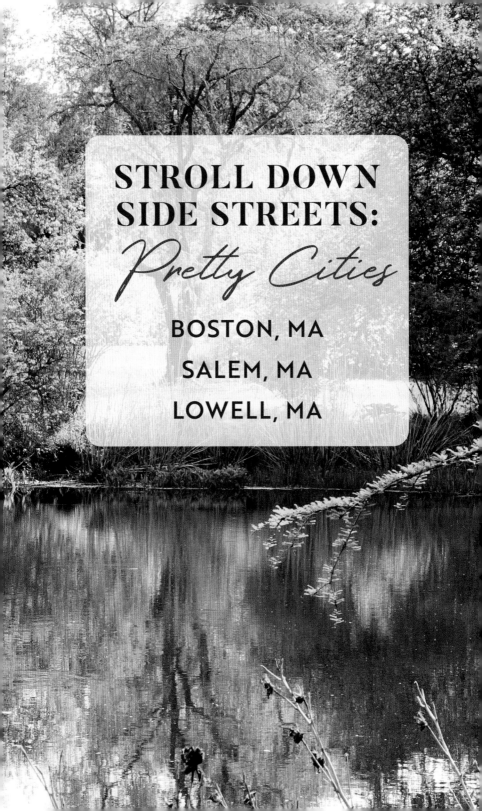

STROLL DOWN SIDE STREETS:
Pretty Cities

BOSTON, MA

SALEM, MA

LOWELL, MA

Boston

BOSTON IS THE LARGEST CITY IN THE COMMONWEALTH OF MASSACHUSETTS AS WELL AS THE STATE CAPITAL.

PAUL REVERE AND SAM ADAMS, Faneuil Hall Marketplace, Harvard University, the world-famous curse-reversing Red Sox—Boston comes with centuries of well-earned swagger. Resettled by Puritans in 1630, Boston is one of America's venerable cities with a rich national legacy. By the 1700s, the New England colonies, along with the British crown, had their eyes on Boston and its citizens. The city was not only a major coastal hub along a lucrative trading route, but it was steadily becoming a place of political unrest and protest against suffocating British rule. On December 16, 1773, these tensions came to a head on Griffin's Wharf when colonists upended more than 300 chests of tea from Britain's East India Tea Company into the harbor. Cemented into the annals of history as the Boston Tea Party, this event would ignite a series of happenings over the next several years that would earn Boston the moniker of the "birthplace of the American Revolution."

But don't let the impressive historical bona fides intimidate you. Boston is so much more than its most spectacular attractions such as the USS *Constitution*, built in 1797 and still sailing, or Fenway Park, the nation's oldest active major-league ballpark. It has evolved to become a leader in technology, industry, art, and education. It is a city proud of its preservation, while simultaneously searching for innovative ways to make its varied urban landscape and exciting offerings accessible and relevant to visitors and citizens alike. I may be biased, but to me, Boston has the superior advantage of existing as several prime places in one: With its green spaces, city neighborhoods and urban features, and harbor coastline within casting distance of the Atlantic Ocean, Boston is the Swiss Army knife of New England cities.

There are no shortage of great ways to experience this lovable, proudly scruffy city. From many types of walking tours to our very fun Boston Duck Tours, giving you the best of land and water sightseeing from the comfort of a safe, amphibious vehicle, any visitor can take in a lot even if they only have a few hours to spare. Here I want to take you just "off the beaten path" to introduce you to some locales and features that highlight a different side of Boston's indelible character, places where pockets of the city's quiet wonder and delightful charm are on full display. There is some wonderful unexpected tranquility and sweetness stowed away in Boston's vibrant urban atmosphere—if you know where to train your gaze and point your feet.

THE EMBRACE, MLK MEMORIAL ON THE COMMON
Freedom Plaza, Boston Common (T access on the Green Line, Park Street)

The Common is to Boston what Central Park is to New York City. It is not only the oldest public park in the nation, but it is the city's largest and most popular green space. Since its inception in 1634, the Common has remained an epicenter of recreation and social and political activity. The harsh New England winters won't keep people from lacing up and skating on the Common's Frog Pond or gripping mugs of hot chocolate to attend the annual holiday tree-lighting ceremony. During more temperate months, the Common is full of Frisbee-players, dog-walkers, bucket-drummers, food-vendors, and plenty of lazy-day-book-and-bench-perchers. Spread a blanket and enjoy a summer performance by the Commonwealth Shakespeare Company or spend time getting to know many of its historical features such as the Granary Burial Ground, which dates back to 1660—the Common is one of those infinitely versatile spaces year-round.

In keeping with Boston's rebellious roots, the Common has been a site for civic gatherings (some peaceful, some not) since the 1700s. British soldiers made the Common their encampment during the occupation of Boston in 1775. Two years later, spectacular fireworks bloomed over the Common in celebration of the Declaration of Independence, July 4, 1777. Fast forward to April 23, 1965, when the Common added a new entry to the history books. On that day the Reverend Dr. Martin Luther King Jr. appeared before more than 20,000 people to speak about racial inequality in and around Boston. Over 50 years later, Dr. King's legacy in Boston has been immortalized with *The Embrace* sculpture.

The Embrace is the most recent addition to public art in the Common, joining other pieces such as the Robert Gould Shaw Memorial for the 54th Massachusetts Voluntary Civil War Infantry and the playful Brewer Fountain.

Designed by artist Hank Willis Thomas and Mass Design Group, the memorial was inspired by a photo of Dr. King and his wife, Coretta Scott King, embracing upon learning the news Dr. King would be awarded the Nobel Peace Prize. Thomas's piece speaks to universal themes of compassion, acceptance, and community. Dr. King's guiding beliefs about the power of connection to transcend racial differences, to connect with one another, are

A short walk from the Park Street T (subway) stop, the bronze *Embrace* casts a striking scene within the Common's natural setting.

The Memorial Day Flag Garden is a moving scene and beautiful way to honor Massachusetts citizens who gave for their country.

also conveyed through the depiction of the figure's hands and arms.

The sculpture is located in a patch of the Common designated the 1965 Freedom Plaza. A circular area of granite stone surrounds the memorial, patterned in a way to evoke African-American quilt-making traditions. The Plaza also commemorates 69 local civil rights leaders active between 1950 and 1970. Granite benches invite visitors to sit and reflect; the curved stone walls provide a sense of intimacy, an invitation to gather closer to the memorial itself and one another.

At first glance, *The Embrace*'s design appears simplistic, but spend some time walking in and around the piece, studying the astonishing attention to fine details, and absorbing it from many different perspectives, and you'll quickly find this sculpture is as complex and fascinating as the couple behind its creation.

MEMORIAL DAY FLAG GARDEN—BOSTON COMMON
Display begins at the Soldiers and Sailors Monument on Boston Common

Another unique event on the Common happens every Memorial Day when red, white, and blue "blooms" appear in the form of the Memorial Day Flag Garden. This hometown tradition was begun in 2010 by members of the Massachusetts Military Heroes Fund. Each year volunteers "plant" more than 37,000 flags to commemorate the Massachusetts service people who paid the ultimate sacrifice in conflicts from the Revolutionary War to the present.

The Flag Garden fans out downward from the top of the hill of the Soldiers and Sailors Monument, covering the Common's gently sloped green.

People can support the work of the Massachusetts Military Heroes Fund year-round by sponsoring a flag. The stunning display can be viewed from many angles, and even with slender ropes to mark the garden's parameters, there is ample access. Visitors can easily move throughout the installation, paying respects and taking time to reflect. The Flag Garden is a singular and unforgettable way to acknowledge the past while remaining in the present.

THE PUBLIC GARDEN

The Public Garden is located west of Boston Common. It is bordered by Charles Street, Arlington Street, Boylston Street, and Boston Common.

Walking through the lush, tranquil grounds of Boston Public Garden today, it's hard to imagine the 24 acres were once a stretch of squishy, sandy mudflats (which probably did not smell so pleasant in the heat of Boston in August!). By the 1800s, the city's plan to fill in the flats was underway with considerable debate about what the land should be used for. Fortunately, the proposal of a graveyard was robustly defeated (1,632 to 176); instead, the city accepted a bid by Boston philanthropist Horace Gray in 1837 to transform the acreage into a beautifully curated park. Two years later, America's first botanical garden opened its gates, christened the Boston Public Garden.

In the decades following its official opening, the Public Garden has undergone numerous changes and developments. All of these additional elements

Established in 1859, the 4-acre pond is the garden's centerpiece. Swimming allowed for friendly waterfowl only.

have been lovingly and carefully chosen and established to maintain the integrity of one of Boston's most treasured spaces.

For instance, on any given late-spring or summer day you can find a line of people waiting to take a leisurely lap around the garden's pond nestled in the wings of one of the iconic Swan Boats.

The brainchild of local businessman Robert Paget, the Swan Boats design was inspired by *Lohengrin*, a Wagner opera where a knight crosses a river in a swan-drawn boat to defend the honor of a princess. Whether or not 19th-century Bostonians felt chivalrous paddling around the Public Garden's lagoon in Paget's Swan Boats we'll never know. But the fact that the boats, run by a fourth generation of the Paget family, continue to delight guests from all over the world every season is living proof of the enduring joy brought about by Robert Paget's simple vision to help people fully enjoy the garden's pond.

The garden's overall design was created by George F. Meacham with the paths and garden beds planned by city engineer James Slade and forester John Galvin. Easily accessible paved walkways loop around the green space populated with diverse tree species that range from English oak to weeping pagodas and dawn redwoods. The Garden has stayed very true to its

Below: A Public Garden staple, the Swan Boats have been delighting paddlers young and old for nearly 150 years. Opposite: Tulips flourish around the George Washington statue, bringing a touch of the Netherlands to Massachusetts.

Mrs. Mallard and her ducklings are often outfitted with festive, seasonal ware throughout the year.

19th-century roots as a place where people could enjoy promenading and socializing among a lovely natural setting. In addition, flower beds are expertly cultivated throughout the grounds to showcase seasonal blooms.

The Public Garden also features its share of public art with various statues scattered throughout the space. One of the most famous pieces is the *Make Way for Ducklings* sculpture created by local artist Nancy Schon. Based on Robert McCloskey's award-winning children's book of the same name, Schon's rendering of Mrs. Mallard and her ducklings greets guests at the garden's Charles and Beacon Streets entrance.

On any given day in the Public Garden you can find musicians busking, artists capturing the beauty of the surroundings, and people from all over the world who've come to experience this gorgeously tranquil spot for themselves.

BEACON HILL

Beacon Hill is a neighborhood bounded by Storrow Drive and Cambridge, Bowdin, Park, and Beacon Streets. It also borders Boston Common and is a short walk from the Park Street T station or the Charles MGH T stop.

With its cobblestone streets and 19th-century lampposts, Boston's Beacon Hill neighborhood could easily pass for a scene in a Charles Dickens novel. Initially established in the mid-1600s, Beacon Hill was not always the upscale locale that it is today. In fact, as the city was undergoing its own growing pains in the 17th and 18th centuries, the Beacon Hill area was used for military drills and livestock grazing. The neighborhood would eventually become home to such affluent residents as singer Carly Simon and financial and business mogul Jack Welch, but you would never guess it from its relatively humble beginnings as a section for sailors, blacksmiths, and others characterized as working class "undesirables."

A transformation in Beacon Hill's geography along with the influence of the renowned 18th-century architect, Charles Bulfinch, changed everything for the Hill. In 1795, flush off his design of the new Massachusetts State House, located at the top of Beacon Hill, Bulfinch worked with city developers to create an updated urban design for this neighborhood, which was becoming badly needed in the face of Boston's overcrowding.

Four years later, the Beacon Hill that exists today with its stately Colonial Revival, Greek Revival, and Federal-style mansions began to take shape.

Beacon Hill brownstones in full bloom.

Beacon Hill has surprises and delights nestled in every nook and cranny.

This is one of Boston's oldest and most scenic neighborhoods and also features a shopping and dining boulevard, making it seem like its own tiny hamlet folded up inside of the city. From the picturesque lampposts, a staple feature established in the 19th century and updated throughout the decades, to the charming gardens and courtyards secreted behind wrought-iron gates, every block is imbued with a distinctive, storied atmosphere.

When wandering the Hill, you'll want to keep your eyes open for all sorts of sweet finds, such as Rouvalis Flowers & Gardens. Stop in this staple of Beacon Hill—family-owned and -operated for more than 40 years—for some seasonal blooms to brighten your nest or to simply linger and marvel at the inventive, beautiful outdoor displays.

You'll also want to keep a look out for inspired "scenes" that crop up in the neighborhood throughout the year. Window boxes get the VIP treatment during spring and winter, but autumn is a whole other doorstop-jawdrop kind of festive time as residents try to outdo each other with ornate (but tasteful!) entryway extravaganzas.

Any time of year is a good time to grab some to-go greenery from Rouvalis.

From as early as the 1840s, Beacon Hill was a location that especially appealed to the "1-percenters" of the period. Renowned homeowners from Louisa May Alcott and Robert Frost to Senator John Kerry and Uma Thurman have all taken up residence on the Hill. Some were lucky enough to live in Louisburg Square, a tiny exclusive enclave within Beacon Hill. Greek Revival–style houses built between 1834 and 1847 look out over cobblestone walkways, bisected by a private park.

But there is another, rather unusual, celebrity lurking in the gently sloping red-bricked streets of Beacon Hill: Acorn Street.

Established around 1795, Acorn Street was originally named Kitchen Street after the small row houses occupied by cooks, coachmen, maids, and others in service of Boston's wealthy families. With its carpet of rare, original cobblestones and its classic American Federal-style brick homes, Acorn Street is not only considered one of the most fetching streets in the country, it is also among the most photographed. Acorn Street is still a residential area. Be respectful and mindful when taking your captures of this charming avenue.

When you're ready to leave the colorful window boxes and lovely stoops in the rear view, head down off the Hill to Charles Street, where you'll find shops, dining, and even more eye-catching elements in this timeless part of Boston.

Among the many stores along Charles Street, you will want to single out some time to get lost in the lovely Beacon Hill Books & Café. This five-story renovated brownstone is outfitted with darling features such as a working train that runs along the rooms in the children's section and a basement-level cafe that opens up onto a sweet courtyard. It's a space that is every book lover's dream, and it is hard not to imagine running into Louisa May Alcott sprawled upon one of the store's many cushioned window seats, scheming a new novel into being.

Beacon Hill is criminally lovely and she knows it! Turn down any street and you'll be greeted with something new to uncover on every old block. Exploring the rich history of this neighborhood alone offers plenty of discoveries to fill a satisfying day spent in Boston and even more reason to plan a return visit.

Treasured finds hiding in plain sight.

BACK BAY, MAGNOLIA SEASON

The Back Bay is a neighborhood bordered by the Charles River to the north, the Massachusetts Turnpike to the south, the Public Garden to the east, and Charlesgate East to the west.

Gradually cultivated between 1858 and 1900, Boston's Back Bay design was inspired by 19th-century Parisian urban planning with attention to long, wide boulevards and interspersed with green space and trees. The elegant blocks that make up the neighborhood are populated with what is largely considered to be the finest representation of Victorian townhouses in the country. On any ordinary day, there is plenty to gawk at with these regal residences and their eye-catching architec-

Magnolias bring big beauty to this Back Bay block.

tural flourishes. But when spring arrives, transom windows and porticos play second fiddle to dazzling, dizzying clouds of pink and white magnolia blooms orbiting doorways and levitating from front yards up and down the streets of the Back Bay. It is worth timing a trip to the city in early to mid-April just to experience this one-of-a-kind magnolia magic.

The magnolias exist thanks to a spark of genius by a woman named Laura Dwight. Laura looked around her street on Commonwealth Avenue in the Back Bay and decided she did not like what she saw: crumbling front stoops, broken gates, dirt and litter patches passing for gardens and flower beds. It was 1963. Unbeknownst to Laura, she was about to turn her desire to create a cleaner, more inviting place to live for everyone in the neighborhood into an enduring beautification movement lasting 50 years and counting.

Both an activist and a naturalist at heart, Laura came up with a simple idea: plant trees to give front yards added curb appeal and to incentivize homeowners to keep their stoops and frontage maintained.

Opposite: A wreath of pink draws you into one of the many brownstones in the Back Bay.

Win/win! First, she researched various varieties and settled upon a species of magnolias that could withstand Boston's chilly spring climate. Then Laura pitched her plan the old-fashioned way, by going door-to-door: Want to turn your front yard into a gorgeous pink dreamscape? For a nominal fee—$8 for a small tree and $20 for a larger, slightly more established tree—Laura would provide all planting materials and labor. Literally, just add water and voilà! Nature on demand.

And not only did Laura's ingenious eco-activism take off, but it inspired others to gift trees to friends who lived on adjacent streets. Zoom ahead more than 5 decades, with over 100 magnolias on Commonwealth Avenue alone, and many additional years of new planting throughout the Back Bay, and the result is a floral marvel to astound your eyes and delight your winter-weary soul.

Walking the city blocks in spring is like meandering through a tunnel made of petals and the promise of the warmth and hope the season brings. Every few feet provides a reason to stop, look up, and marvel at the exquisite blooms climbing up the sides of red-bricked buildings, coyly entwining themselves around wrought-iron balconies.

Organizations such as the Garden Club of the Back Bay have taken on the care and maintenance of the trees, including planting new ones throughout the neighborhood. Their hard work combined with ongoing participation from Back Bay homeowners has ensured that what began as Laura Dwight's modest efforts will continue to grow and provide an annual spring spectacular for generations to come.

COMMONWEALTH AVENUE MALL
484 Commonwealth Ave., Boston, MA; access at the western edge of the
Public Garden or via the parallel streets of the Back Bay

Winston Churchill called the Commonwealth Avenue Mall "the grandest boulevard in North America." Enormously proud of their city, Bostonians would say Mr. Churchill was "wicked right." Just about anyone who takes a stroll down the idyllic tree-lined promenade will admit it's a fantastic use of urban space: a surprisingly quiet corridor that softens the city buzz.

Like most things in Boston, there is more to the story of what appears to be a modest stretch of city blocks. Throughout the 1800s urban planners continued to develop and fill the marshy

Opposite: File under bloom POW!

The likeness of Founding Father Alexander Hamilton, installed on the Mall in 1865, welcomes guests beneath the green.

areas of Boston most prone to ocean flooding, creating neighborhoods like the Back Bay. The preeminent architect of the time period, Arthur Gilman, saw the Back Bay forming in its infancy and fiercely advocated for the construction of a grand, grassy mall. This, Gilman believed, would not only serve as a central axis in terms of layout and design, but would create the kind of sophisticated sweeping promenade popularized in France. Class and style like the Parisians, but in keeping with Boston's rougharound-the-collar charm. How could Gilman lose?

Luckily he didn't and the Mall was built between 1858 and 1870. It occupied a 32-acre lane connecting the new, elegant Back Bay with the Public Garden and other smaller green spaces south of the city. It also became a model of the ideal boulevard used by civic designers and planners all over America. Moreover, this additional urban path brought other benefits to the already very attractive Back Bay area. Nineteenth-century Bostonians not only enjoyed a safe place to walk and socialize, they also used the Mall for a particular kind of play: the wide, straight, even terrain of the Mall and its crushed stone made it ideal for carriage races and parades.

In Gilman's meticulous planning he stipulated that the grand mansions lining either side of the Mall had to be set back 20 feet from the property line to give ample space to the 200-foot-wide expanse that included the primary Mall and its two ancillary streets for motorists. The effect makes the Mall feel blissfully insular. The exquisite variety of shade trees—green ash, maple, and elm—that form the Mall's leafy passageway enhances the sense that even in the present day you are ambling through another time entirely.

The Mall is more than just a place to relax or socialize; it has evolved into another one of Boston's vibrant art spaces. Sculptures were not originally part of the Mall's design. Instead they were gradually added in as early as 1865 through to the 21st century.

Many of the more modern pieces on the Mall reflect a style of public art that is meant to be engaging as well as introspective. The Vendome Firefighters' Memorial is a moving example of this approach. A collaboration between sculptor Theodore Clausen and landscape architect Peter White, this piece is a stirring tribute to the nine firefighters who died on June 17, 1972, fighting the Hotel Vendome fire.

With its textured elements and inviting, curved shape, Clausen and White's design draws visitors close.

The Boston Women's Memorial, added to the Mall in 2003, is another particularly striking art installation. As early as 1992, the Boston Women's Commission began raising funds and fielding proposals to create a monument addressing the lack of women represented in Boston's public art. A space on the Mall at the Fairfield-Gloucester blocks was set aside and the commission worked for more than a decade to continue acquiring support and choose the artist. New York sculptor Meredith Bergmann is the creator behind a dynamic scene featuring three women with ties to the Bay State and deeply held beliefs about social justice, equality, and the power of both pen and voice.

The memorial features Abigail Adams, born in Weymouth, Massachusetts, and wife of President John Adams; Lucy Stone from Brookfield, Massachusetts, a passionate abolitionist; and Phillis Wheatley, an enslaved woman brought from Africa to Boston who learned to read and write, becoming a literary prodigy and publishing a book of poems.

Part of what makes Bergmann's sculptures profound is the way their design encourages people to encounter the women rather than admire them from a distance. People of all ages get up close and personal with these figures, posing with them for photos, circling around them to read the inscriptions and look closely at their expertly rendered features.

Arthur Gilman succeeded in bringing something special and built to withstand the changes to a busy urban center like Boston when he envisioned the idyllic pathway that would become the Commonwealth Avenue Mall more than a century ago. When the leaves fall and the bare trees stretch their arms out over the Mall, city workers wreathe the branches in warm, white lights and suddenly both guests and residents find a whole new reason to walk the Mall.

Meredith Bergmann's likeness of early feminist Abigail Adams (standing) and abolitionist Lucy Stone (writing) depicts these women in their roles as active members of society.

THE BOSTON PUBLIC LIBRARY
700 Boylston St., Boston, MA

You don't have to be on the hunt for that hot *New York Times* bestseller or in pursuit of cutting-edge research to need a reason to pop into the central branch of the Boston Public Library (BPL). Ornate ceiling frescos, incredible murals, and beautiful sculptures and design details throughout the building—if you didn't know it, you might think you were in an art museum.

They say it takes a village to raise a child; in Boston the same could be said about building a central library. Several influential Bostonians in the early 1800s publicly advocated for the consolidation of the city's various library facilities. After many stops and starts, which included a major donation from the New York City tycoon, John Jacob Astor, the general court of the

Meredith Bergmann's startling likeness of Phillis Wheatley in artful, meaningful contemplation evokes the depth and richness of a fascinating woman.

Commonwealth of Massachusetts issued a statute in 1848 to create a citywide library.

The first building to house collections was a modest former schoolhouse located on Mason Street, which opened its doors to the public in March of 1854. Bostonians have a long, proud relationship with bookish pursuits and seeking out scholarly advantage. It was immediately apparent that this structure was no match for the library's collection of 16,000 volumes. A new, larger location opened on Boylston Street in 1858, but in only 2 decades the library was bursting at the spines once again and Trustees lobbied the state legislature for the kind of real estate footprint befitting Boston's embarrassment of literary riches. Where might such a plot of land exist? How about all that space around the newly filled Back Bay neighborhood, suggested the Trustees. On April 22, 1880, the state granted this request, signing over property at the corner of Dartmouth and Boylston Streets.

Yellow Siena marble bathes the lobby in inviting warmth.

The new building's design went to the firm of McKim, Mead & White with architect Charles Follen McKim assigned as the principal on the project. McKim based his vision of "a palace for the people" on the Bibliothèque Sainte-Geneviève in Paris, built in 1850. He also drew inspiration from Italian and Mediterranean architectural influences in other elements from the shape of windows to the style and placement of sconces and sculptures. The sculptor Bela Pratt created the two figures for the library's stepped promenade: *Science* holding a globe and *Art* with a palette and brush.

Opposite: Despite its imposing and ornately embellished exterior, the Boston Public Library is a sanctuary of art, learning, and culture for all. It currently houses 23 million items that include maps, drawings, manuscripts, letters, and other original works dating back as early as the 10th century.

These library patrons are gentle giants at heart.

Before a guest encounters her first bookshelf, she's welcomed into an atmosphere that pulses with history, intellect, art, culture, innovation, and a sense of what some of the most remarkable minds from every sphere of knowledge can accomplish.

The impressive staircase hall guides patrons into the heart of the library. However, every good story involves a quest, and a journey to the library's vast rewards of art and knowledge is no different. All visitors must first pass by and pay special tribute to the library's guardians: a pair of marble lions.

Created by sculptor Louis Saint-Gaudens, these lions honor the 2nd and 20th Civil War volunteer infantries from Massachusetts. Surviving members of the regiments funded the memorials. Under a deadline to complete the pieces for the library's opening, Saint-Gaudens was forced to deliver the lions before he could perform a final polish and refining on them. The regiment survivors found they preferred the "unpolished, raw" look as a more fitting tribute to the men who gave their lives for their country. They strongly contested both McKim and library trustees who wanted to alter the statues and succeeded in keeping the lions "rough." After the new Boston Public Library opened in 1895, patrons began a tradition of rubbing the lions' tails for good luck that continues today.

On every floor and in nearly every room, the BPL is overrun with artwork and murals from some of the most famous painters from all over the world. Encircling the grand staircase is the work of Pierre Puvis de Chavannes, a French painter known as one of the most extraordinary muralists of the 19th century. The panels in the BPL are his only mural pieces outside of France. Each panel was painted on Belgian linen in Paris, then shipped to Boston for installation. Though Puvis never saw his art installed, he was

Sargent incorporated many belief systems in these works: from Egyptian and Assyrian to Judaism and Christianity.

given a sample of the Siena marble used for the room as a way to base his color scheme and design.

Another renowned artist featured throughout the library is John Singer Sargent. The third floor has become an art gallery of Sargent's murals, which he spent 29 years in total painting. Though Sargent lived and traveled extensively in Europe, he retained his strong ties to Boston. Sargent created the panels for his mural, titled *The Triumph of Religion*, in England and traveled with them to the city over the course of four installation phases. Gilded molding makes the painted figures seem to glimmer; ruby and scarlet hues fill the walls of the hall with its gray stone floor with captivating color.

One of the most iconic and lived-in rooms in the BPL is Bates Hall, a hushed hall that carries a soothing aura of contemplation and concentration.

The second-floor reading and study room was named after Joshua Bates, one of the library's first benefactors. Bates was a wealthy banker from Weymouth, Massachusetts. In 1852 as plans for the library were coming together, Bates donated $50,000 for construction and an additional $50,000 to purchase

Whether studying, working, or poring over a volume for pleasure, Bates Hall is warm and welcoming.

books. He remained one of the library's staunch supporters who fiercely advocated for the institution's services and resources and that they always remain "free to all."

Bates Hall features another one of McKim's staggering architectural feats on display in the form of its 50-foot-high barrel vault coffered ceiling. All the elements of this elegant, but accessible, space coalesce to make even the casual visitor feel as if she were transported to a library on another side of the world or even in the pages of an iconic storybook.

Libraries have always been about more than books. They strive to be inclusive places for learning, discovery, and community connection. Boston's Public Library offers all of this (and more) housed in a space custom made for engaging and inspiring every person's potential.

THE CHARLES RIVER ESPLANADE (THE ESPLANADE)

The Esplanade runs along the Charles River from the Longfellow Bridge to the Harvard Bridge. It can be accessed via the Charles MGH T stop on the Red Line. It can also be accessed on foot from the Beacon Hill and Back Bay neighborhoods.

Boston's green spaces are expertly woven within the fabric of the city, and the Charles River Esplanade is no exception. This 3-mile stretch of walkways and footbridges winds along the historic Charles River, an 80-mile stretch of waterway that runs through numerous Massachusetts towns before meeting with the Atlantic. The Charles River, originally called *Quinobequin* (a Native American term meaning "meandering"), was once one of the nation's main

Springtime paints the Esplanade in sweet hues with numerous cherry trees lining pathways.

suppliers of hydropower for industrialization. Currently, the Charles makes the most of its retirement as one of the most popular waterways for sailing, kayaking, canoeing, and even paddleboarding. Every fall the banks of the Charles River fill as if it were midnight in Times Square as people travel from all over the world to watch the famous Head of the Charles, the world's largest long-distance regatta. However, out of the water, the Charles River Esplanade offers another, unexpectedly delightful, unique city "park" to explore, discover, and enjoy.

The Esplanade has come a long way since its dedication as the unfortunately named Boston Embankment in 1910. As Boston city planners aggressively shaped the city during the 18th century, they found themselves constantly contending with the fact that every intervention into Boston's novel urban geography (those salty, slimy mudflats again!) created a different set of planning problems or, in some cases, entirely new pieces of landscape. This was partly the case with the stretch of property that would eventually become the Esplanade.

The Charles River Esplanade teems with plenty of outdoor fun and beautiful, eye-catching views.

Every view of the Charles River along the Esplanade is a winner.

In the early 1900s, landscape architect Charles Eliot led the efforts to dam the Charles River basin. By this time the river was still tidal, which meant that at each low tide the residents of the shiny, affluent Back Bay neighborhood were doused with the wretched odors of waste water. The Charles River Dam Project transformed the tidal flats into a wide basin, keeping the water level constant. The resulting thoroughfare skirting the Charles was little more than a poorly maintained promenade—no trees, landscaping, or recreational opportunities. There was not much reason for citizens to use the space other than to walk from one part of the city to another.

Thankfully, landscape architect Arthur Shurcliff intervened, setting the land on its destined course to become one of the most beloved areas in the city. During the 1920s and 1930s, Shurcliff oversaw major improvements: adding in trees and other perennial bushes and flowers; building out a lagoon; constructing scenic plazas and landings for boats; erecting playgrounds; and eventually, in 1941 building a dedicated pavilion for outdoor music. The historic Hatch Memorial Shell is home to the famous Boston Pops Orchestra. If you're lucky enough to be in town on the Fourth of July, pack a blanket and snacks and head to the Esplanade early in the day to score a prime spot to hear the fabled orchestra perform its annual Independence Day concert.

Every generation stewarding the Esplanade has continued to implement improvements and updated beautification efforts. Every spring, the Esplanade blushes pink with the blooming of more than 1,500 cherry trees gifted from Japan in the 1980s. Cross softly over one of the many footbridges and you just might catch a heron nosing around for a snack in one of the Esplanade's reedy banks. Community Boating, a nonprofit and Boston mainstay since 1936, provides boating rentals and lessons right from the Esplanade's edge.

Head to the Esplanade for recreation, relaxation, or to find inspiration and solitude along the shores of the mighty Charles. Fun, versatile, and close to other favorite city spots such as the Back Bay and Newbury Street, the Esplanade is one of the best ways to get your fix of many different natural elements while staying within city limits.

GRAFFITI ALLEY
565-567 Massachusetts Ave., Cambridge, MA

Tucked between two buildings there's a whole museum just steps away from the Central Square T stop.

One of the most instagrammable spots in Cambridge, Massachusetts, Graffiti Alley is endlessly inventive, wildly creative, and always different.

The art-based alley was the quirky concept of friends Geoff Hargadon, a local artist, and Gary Strack, a restauranteur. Strack owned Brick & Mortar, an eatery that shared a wall with a dark, narrow alley that was little more than any typical, dirty city corridor. But in 2007, Strack and Hargadon decided to change all of that, inviting 30 artists from America and Canada to paint in the alley. The only rules: unleash your imagination and have fun. Word quickly spread about their inspired use of this unremarkable, gritty space and soon artists from all over were flocking to create on brick canvas.

Since then, Graffiti Alley (officially known as Richard B. "Rico" Modica Way) has served as a home and playful space to artists of all types and styles including some well-known figures such as Shepard Fairey, Momo, and Enzo & Nio. As one of the only legal places to paint in the city, Graffiti Alley is a sought-after piece of urban canvas.

Ready, set . . . ART!

A walk through this evolving outdoor art gallery is a shock to the eyes and mind in the best possible way. There are no set times when artists can create, so drop by often. You might just happen upon the next Christina Angelina or Banksy in action.

THE BRATTLE BOOK SHOP
9 West St., Boston, MA

From legendary writers such as Robert Frost and Sylvia Plath to contemporary storytellers such as Susan Minot and Dennis Lehane, Boston has always thrived as a literary town. Even Charles Dickens spent time in the city in 1867. He resided at the upscale Parker House hotel in downtown Boston, which is still operating and a popular stop on "haunted Boston" tours, for 5 months while he regaled area readers and dodged the equivalent of 19th-century paparazzi. Boston is for book lovers. And a great way to get to know any town in general is to spend some time roaming the stacks at any one of its independent bookstores. That's where the Brattle Book

Between hours, outdoor market volumes rest in colorful, storybook carrels.

Shop comes in. This store is a perfect blend of history, diversity, and scruffy charm—just like Boston.

Though the Brattle Book Shop has been in existence since 1825, it has had a curiously nomadic past. Just like the great volumes that line its shelves, the Brattle Book Shop has been passed from location to location since the early 1960s. It was first installed in the 19th century in the Cornhill section of Boston, an area known for its wide array of booksellers and publishing houses. By 1962 the shop had landed on nearby Brattle Street, but a major city redevelopment plan in that area demolished a number of streets to make way for what would become City Hall Plaza. It wasn't until 1984 that the wandering Brattle Book Shop cooled its heels at its permanent spot on West Street, not far from the theater district.

All those books were never going to move themselves, right? In 1949 the store was purchased by the Gloss family, who continue to run the store today. Kenneth Gloss, a second-generation family member, manages what is considered America's oldest antiquarian bookstore. Gloss is not only a

legacy owner, he is also an antiquarian book expert and appraiser who has been featured on the *Antiques Roadshow* program and conducted appraisals for universities such as Harvard and Tufts, as well as for the FBI. That sounds like a story made for the shelves of the Brattle itself!

As you might have guessed, the bookstore packs an impressive amount of literary punch in its modest walls: over 250,000 items that range from books, maps, and prints to postcards and ephemeral materials. The third floor houses first editions and other collectible pieces in its rare book room. But if you can't afford that first edition of *To Kill a Mockingbird*, don't worry. There's plenty of treasures waiting in the store's outdoor book market in the lot next to the main shop. Weather depending, bookstalls fill the small lot year-round where you can pick up an obscure or wildly popular read on the cheap.

The Brattle Book Shop has hopefully found its cozy forever niche on West Street. It's close to the Downtown Crossing shopping district but offers something more than the average retailer: rarities, treasures, and unique finds for passionate page-turners of all ages.

THE ROSE FITZGERALD KENNEDY GREENWAY

Because the Greenway runs through the length of Boston from the North End to the South Station area, you can access the park on foot along stops at every MBTA line (Red, Green, Orange, Blue, Silver); from the commuter rail at both North and South Stations; and with Bluebike sharing stations.

What began as a not-so-simple fix for Boston's not-so-simple-or-fun traffic congestion ultimately became a new jewel in the crown of the city's expanding natural territories. The Rose Fitzgerald Kennedy Greenway gathers some of the best of what Boston has to offer with food trucks, beer and wine gardens, artisan market vendors, and family-friendly events and activities spread along a vibrant outdoor 1.5-mile plaza. The remarkably designed Greenway bisects the length of the city from the edge of the North End down to Chinatown with downtown Boston on one side and the beautiful, scenic harbor on the other. In another development company's hands, the Greenway might have easily become just another place for high rises and restaurants, missing this golden, or green, opportunity entirely.

In 1991 Boston undertook the most ambitious civic project in the history of the city, known as "The Big Dig." This project was decades in the making since

Nature plays a starring role along the meandering Greenway.

Dare to dash through the Greenway's fun Rings Fountain.

the early 1950s as the commuting traffic along Boston's Central Artery—its primary, heavily gridlocked highway—continued to worsen. Civic planners proposed sinking the Central Artery below ground and creating a massive tunnel to alleviate the issue. The Big Dig was one of the most complicated, expensive, technologically difficult projects in the history of both Boston and the United States. When the last tunnel tile was fixed in place and the final support beam tightened and tested, the highway disappeared underground. Left in its place was a prime piece of new real estate. Fortunately, community and political leaders aligned to propose turning the land into another type of green space. Thanks to the joint efforts of the Massachusetts Turnpike Authority, the Commonwealth of Massachusetts, the City of Boston, and numerous civic and nonprofit organizations, in October of 2008, the Rose Kennedy Greenway held its inaugural ribbon cutting and welcomed thousands of visitors to its gently roaming pathways and lovely garden plots.

The Greenway is named after Rose Fitzgerald Kennedy, the matriarch of the famous Kennedy family. Rose had deep roots in Boston. She was born in the North End and raised her family in Massachusetts not far from the city. Rose maintained an active presence in Boston philanthropic, social, and civic endeavors related to the city's beautification and diversity initiatives. Her son, the venerable Senator Edward M. Kennedy, was an instrumental supporter of the Greenway. It seemed only fitting to name Boston's newest green addition after a woman who devoted her life to the growth and care of a city that meant so much to her.

Take a spin on one of these whimsical carousel pals.

Unfolding in what appears to be a continuous series of walkways, the Greenway contains a series of discrete, cultivated green spaces within its borders. The Auntie Kay and Uncle Frank Chin Park anchors the southern end of the Greenway with design elements and details inspired by nearby Chinatown. Next up is the Dewey Square Park, situated between Congress and Summer Streets along Atlantic Avenue, close to Boston's train depot, South Station, and the Financial District. Sprawling lawn areas dotted with tables and chairs make Dewey Square Park the perfect lunchtime spot. More cultivated gardens and lines of leafy trees populate the Fort Channel Park portion of the Greenway, located between Oliver and Congress Streets along Atlantic Avenue.

The Wharf District Parks are probably the most frequented part of the Greenway. They join Boston's highly touristed Faneuil Hall with both the Financial District and Boston Harbor areas. Here you'll find weekend vendors, concerts, fitness classes and meet-ups, as well as rotating public art installations. Designed by the firms of EDAW and Copley Wolff Design, the Wharf District Parks present as three open lawn spaces or "rooms" surrounded by plantings and other seasonal greenery. A focal point of this area is Rings Fountain, a very fun courtyard splash zone for kids of all ages.

There is always something new and marvelous to see along the Greenway. In 2013 the Greenway Conservancy raised funds to install the Greenway Carousel.

This one-of-a-kind kid- and adult-friendly amusement park staple is a beautiful and popular addition to the Greenway. Classic carousel characters are reimagined with a Boston-centric twist. The hand-carved fish, sea turtles, hares, and more are based on the wildlife native to Boston Harbor and the area and inspired by drawings submitted by Boston schoolchildren. Since its installation, the Greenway Carousel has seen more than 10,000 visits a year.

Shop, nibble, wander, wonder, laze-repeat. The Greenway is just the right amount of casual fun and play when you're in town.

HARBORWALK TO FAN PIER PARK

Access the harborwalk via the Boston Marriott Long Wharf Hotel (296 State St., Boston, MA) and follow the boardwalk along the water to Fan Pier Park.

There's literally a whole other side to Boston to fall in love with: its magnificent harbor and ocean setting. Taking a stroll along the harborwalk to Fan

Pier Park is a fantastic way to catch some unique views of the city and experience a bit of the seaport, one of Boston's up-and-coming revitalized sections.

The Greenway wasn't the only gift left by The Big Dig. Sinking the Central Artery opened up roadways and public transportation networks around the seaport and the South Boston Waterfront sections. With the area more easily accessible by bus, subway, car, and even water taxi, the seaport district was suddenly lit with a desirable new sheen to developers. In 2010, Boston mayor Thomas Menino announced plans for a redesign of 1,000 acres of the South Boston Waterfront that would transform it into a go-to destination for work in cutting-edge industries and an exciting, unique place to live. Mayor Menino informally christened this nascent part of Boston the Innovation District. In the years that have followed, the seaport has lived up to its new designation and then some. Beautifully refurbished residential buildings share space with businesses in the mobile, tech, and clean energy spaces. Upscale eateries, bars, and boutique retail have created another shopping and social hotspot in the city.

But the creation of Fan Pier Park put the seaport in a whole other level of lovely. Just a few years before Mayor Menino announced his seaport project, a group of developers called The Fallon Company had their sights set on the same area. More specifically, the group had zeroed in on a 9-acre portion close to the harbor, which, at the time, was underutilized as parking lots. The Fallon Company saw the site's potential and by 2015 had transformed the space into a spacious promenade offering incredible views of the Boston skyline.

You can easily find your way to Fan Pier Park via the harborwalk, which routes along the water, past hotels such as the Boston Harbor Hotel, over the Evelyn Moakley Bridge. From there take your time along the walking path to take in the varied architecture and to read up on Boston's maritime history relayed on informational stanchions along the harbor's edge. You'll want to follow along Fan Pier all the way to the elevated platform. The short climb up the wide steps is worth the eye-catching reward.

Boston's Innovation District is primed to continue evolving into one of the most sought-after places in the city to live, work, and play. Fan Pier Park ensures that longtime residents have a relaxing enclave to retreat to and visitors get a special take on this classic town.

A show-stopping
seaport scene.

NORTH END

The North End can be accessed via the Haymarket T stop (Orange Line) or Aquarium T stop (Blue Line). It is also within easy walking distance of Faneuil Hall Marketplace and the Rose Fitzgerald Kennedy Greenway.

All the charm, culture, and delicacies of Italy without the passport or airport lines await you in the North End of Boston, a tiny, quaint neighborhood (clocking in at 1 square mile) overflowing with Italian cuisine, specialty food markets, cultural festivals, and, of course, a lot of history.

The North End is Boston's oldest residential neighborhood, inhabited since the city was resettled in 1630. Wealthy families as well as artisans and tradespeople

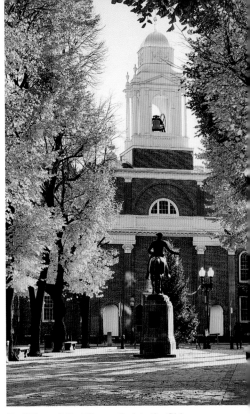

Stroll through Paul Revere Park to the Old North Church to stand at the foot of history.

shared the streets of the North End in the 1700s, and the area unexpectedly became a focus of revolutionary unrest in the years leading up to war. For instance, on August 26, 1765, protestors to the Stamp Act set fire to Lieutenant Governor Thomas Hutchinson's North Square mansion, forcing the panicked governor to escape through his garden (and send a dispatch to England begging for a reassignment). The Old North Church was built in 1723. Fifty years later the church would play a starring role in America's bid for independence. On the night of April 18, 1775, two lanterns dangled in the top of the North Church, signaling that British troops were advancing west by land to capture munitions. Once the lanterns were lit, silversmith and patriot Paul Revere set out on horseback to spread the warning far and wide.

Opposite: In the North End the architecture is as sumptuous as the dishes.; Ciao Roma restaurant is a go-to dining destination in the North End's picturesque North Square.; Pick up the finest imported ingredients for your next special meal at any one of the North End's specialty food shops.

The North End flaunts its festival flare.

The first half of the 19th century brought enormous shifts to the North End. There was a boom in commercial development, which led to dangerously overcrowded conditions. The affluent residents who had been calling the North End home drifted across town to the newly established, highly desirable Beacon Hill neighborhood. But it was the massive waves of Irish, Eastern European Jewish, and Italian immigrants settling in the North End that transformed the neighborhood into the rich cultural center it is today.

Though the North End celebrates a diverse population, it honors its Italian heritage in more than mouth-watering culinary delights. From June through early September, the North End turns extra festive as Italian Americans celebrate numerous feasts such as the Fisherman's Feast, St. Lucy's Feast, and Saint Anthony's Feast. Food vendors pile plates, people gather for parades and speeches, and colorful decorations yawn across the narrow streets. The entire neighborhood feels like one giant block party and everyone is invited.

Block after block in the North End celebrates a sense of old-world traditions thriving in the midst of Boston's fast-growing modern scene. The intoxicating aromas of homemade sauce, sizzling garlic, and fresh baked everything will draw you up Hanover Street, the neighborhood's primary thoroughfare lined with award-winning restaurants and cafes. From there it's easy to pick any street and spend the day roaming around this lovely, scenic section of Boston.

THE ISABELLA STEWART GARDNER MUSEUM
25 Evans Way, Boston, MA

Isabella Stewart Gardner realized she was in a little bit of a pickle: Her art collection was so massive she was running out of room to store it. What a wonderful problem to have! She did the only thing that seemed reasonable to a wealthy Boston socialite at the time. She and her husband, John, decided to build a museum space to house their art and make it available to the viewing public. What a happy solution for everyone! And for more than a century, the Gardner Museum has welcomed generations of patrons into its homey atmosphere to enjoy the incredible art and artifacts lovingly curated by Isabella and John.

Isabella was born into a wealthy New York family. She was sent to the best schools in Paris, which is where she met her future husband, John "Jack" Gardner. The pair wed in 1860 and moved to John's hometown in Boston,

The stunning Italian-inspired grand Courtyard always in perfect bloom at the Gardner Museum.

taking up residence in a spacious brownstone in the city's very fashionable Back Bay neighborhood, which was a wedding gift from her father.

To cope with the tragic loss of their first child, John, who was a little over a year old when he passed away from pneumonia, the Gardners decided to travel abroad. This trip ignited Isabella's passion for travel, which would factor significantly into her enthusiasm for collecting.

As the Gardners settled into life in Boston, Isabella became increasingly involved in its intellectual, social, and philanthropic circles. She attended a lecture by Charles Eliot Norton, the first professor of art history at Harvard University, where they struck up a friendship. Dr. Norton encouraged Isabella to pursue her deeper interest in artifacts, which she did by beginning to acquire rare books and manuscripts. The spark of Isabella's lifelong work had been lit, and people from all over the world would marvel in her rewards.

By the 1880s the Gardners had traveled extensively through Italy and other parts of Europe, amassing a tremendous number of materials from paintings from artists such as Rembrandt, Vermeer, and Titian to relics, tapestries, furniture, and more. All of this added to the Gardners' dilemma of how to manage their embarrassment of beautiful riches. And their idea for a museum was born.

Unfortunately, John did not live to see their shared vision realized, passing away from a stroke in December 1898. His death only made Isabella more determined to move forward to make their dream a reality. Six weeks later, Isabella had purchased a plot of land in the marshy Fens area of Boston and met with architect Willard T. Sears to draw up plans for the museum. Over the next 5 years, Isabella meticulously oversaw every aspect of the museum: from choosing building materials curated from all over the world, especially from Isabella and John's beloved country of Italy, to weighing in on aspects of the design in general. Isabella was so involved that Willard would often quip he was more like the engineer and Isabella the architect. In fact, Willard often found himself in the role of running interference between Isabella (and her many changes and updates) and his beleaguered workers.

Isabella's labor of love and passion for art collecting culminated in 1903 with the official public opening of the Isabella Stewart Gardner Museum. The grand ceremonies included a performance by members of the Boston Symphony Orchestra and light fare that included champagne and doughnuts.

A glimpse of these bright orange beauties is guaranteed to chase away any lingering late-winter chills.

During her lifetime, Isabella also used the museum as her personal residence. She lived in quarters on the fourth floor, which enabled her to remain hands on in the continuous arranging and curating of her ever-expanding collection. Even today, as visitors move from room to room with their novel array of artistic pieces, visitors still feel as if they've been personally invited into her home by Isabella herself. For more than 2 decades, Isabella was an active presence behind the scenes of the museum as a collector as well as out in front as a host to many performances and lectures held at the Gardner. She remained steadfast in her support for the arts until her death in 1924.

Sadly, tragedy would visit Isabella and her art-loving legacy more than 6 decades after she had passed. In the midnight hours of March 18, 1990, 13 works of art were stolen from the Gardner Museum. Two men posing as police officers showed up at the museum claiming to have responded to an alarm. The security guards admitted them. "This is a robbery," the men reportedly said before tying up the guards and getting on with the business at hand. The thieves toured the museum for over an hour, making off with priceless pieces including Rembrandt's *The Storm on the Sea of Galilee*, thought to be his only known seascape. Empty frames hang in the Dutch Room gallery as haunted placeholders waiting for Isabella's magnificent acquisitions to be returned to their rightful place. The art has never been found, but the FBI has continued to offer a reward for any information leading to the recovery of the invaluable treasures.

The Gardner Museum is built to evoke a 15th-century Venetian palace, and nowhere is this more evident than in the building's stunning visual and spatial centerpiece: the Courtyard. Byzantine and Gothic influences join Isabella's Italian tastes to create a gorgeous interior oasis. Museum specialists keep the Courtyard "blooming" year-round, but springtime is when the Courtyard truly dazzles with the annual installation of Isabella's hanging nasturtiums.

Nasturtiums were Isabella's favorite flowers. They bloomed just in time for her birthday, April 14, and their lush, lovely, cheerful tangerine petals made for welcoming faces after long, dreary New England winters. Around 1904, Isabella began the tradition of having the flowers installed in the luxurious courtyard of her beloved museum. It is an ongoing ritual that for many in the area signifies the first happy steps toward warmer days with longer light. It is also simply another kind of work of art adding to the museum's remarkable collection.

For many years, Isabella grew nasturtiums in her greenhouse out in Brookline, Massachusetts. She adored them so much that she began having them "installed" in the Courtyard as early as 1904, and the showstopping tradition has continued since. Spilling out from the third-floor Venetian windows, the 20-foot-long, leggy green vines dangle down the side of the stone balconies, tickling the edges of the stucco walls. Tangerine-colored nasturtiums nestle together in the green thicket, looking delicious enough to lick, though that impulse is frowned upon.

The growing process takes all year, but the nasturtiums are only viable for about 2 weeks after they fully bloom. Making the time and effort to catch this display is worth the effort. Isabella wouldn't want it any other way.

ARNOLD ARBORETUM
125 Arborway, Boston, MA

Free and open to the public, the arboretum is accessible by the MBTA Orange Line Forest Hills stop. There are also a variety of guided tours offered by the staff.

When you hear the phrase "city of Boston," you might think of the Boston Red Sox, the Boston Tea Party, or even Boston cream pies. You probably don't think "sprawling botanical garden." That's exactly why the Arnold Arboretum is such a wonderful, unexpected treasure to the city. Located in the Jamaica Plain and Roslindale neighborhoods on the southwest outskirts of Boston, the Arnold Arboretum is a natural oasis. Any time of the year is an ideal time to slip inside its gates and relish the peace and enjoy exploring the vast and varied landscapes of one of Boston's quietly cherished spots.

Though the arboretum sits slightly apart from its sister green spaces like the Public Garden and the Boston Common, it is very much a continuation of the city's proud commitment to making nature accessible to its citizens. This was very much on the mind of James Arnold, a wealthy merchant from New Bedford, Massachusetts, who had made his fortune in the whaling industry. An agricultural and horticultural enthusiast, Arnold was one of the founders of the New Bedford Horticultural Society and cultivated elaborate varietal gardens around his New Bedford property. When Arnold passed away in 1872, his will stipulated that $100,000 should go toward the "promotion of Horticultural and Agricultural improvements." His estate trustees turned the matter over to a board they felt would be more suited to carrying out Arnold's wishes: The President and Fellows of Harvard College. The group took Arnold's gift and combined it with 120 acres of existing land that had been donated to the college by Benjamin Bussey, another financially successful

merchant and longtime advocate for advancing the science of horticulture. James Arnold's wishes were one step closer to becoming a reality.

The Arnold Arboretum was cultivated slowly over its first 5 years. The arboretum's first director was the botanist Charles Sprague Sargent. In 1877 Sargent commissioned the renowned landscape architect Frederick Law Olmsted to develop paths and discrete access roads. The arboretum's design not only enabled visitors to move through the 281-acre property easily, but it also allowed Sargent and his teams to thoughtfully organize the quickly expanding collections of trees, plants, and flowers.

Plant exploration and scientific research have always comprised the soul of the arboretum. From as early as the 1890s, botanists and horticulturalists from all over America began making contributions to the Arnold. The British botanist Ernest Henry Wilson led six expeditions spanning across China, Japan, and Korea between 1899 and 1919. Many of Wilson's plants continue to flourish and propagate within the arboretum today.

One of the facets that makes the Arnold Arboretum superior is its status as a world-class research facility. There are more than 17,000 species of plants, trees, and flowers populating the arboretum, but one that manages to upstage many of the others: the lilac.

The Arnold is home to more than 400 varieties of lilacs and when they arrive in all their purple, pink, and white splendor, it is a feast for the eyes and a joy for the sweet, sweet senses. Each May since 1908 the arboretum hosts "Lilac Sunday," a designated day to celebrate the power of this humble flower and the one day of the year when picnicking is allowed. Calendar your springtime visit, pack snacks and your favorite blanket, lounge underneath the lush, luxurious fragrant blooms, and don't forget to give a nod of thanks to James Arnold.

Once you start to nose around Boston's crooked cow-path-inspired streets and get a little more familiar with its fascinating history, it's hard not to find a lot to like about this revolutionary town. Even after more than three centuries, Boston is full of surprises—some of them being dreamed up by young minds just finding their footing in the Innovation District and others waiting to be found on the next block, in a corner of green space, or down a technicolor-paint-splattered alleyway by you.

Opposite: When every spot feels like the perfect resting place, it's hard to choose a favorite.; Now that's the best kind of crowd to get lost in.; Tranquility lives in every nook and cranny of the Arnold Arboretum.

Salem

DURING THE FALL MONTHS SALEM IS AN EXTREMELY BUSY TOURIST DESTINATION, ON THE NORTH SHORE OF MASSACHU-SETTS AT THE MOUTH OF THE NAUMKEAG RIVER. THE CITY OF SALEM WEBSITE POSTS UPDATES ON WHERE TO PARK IF YOU ARE COMING BY CAR AS WELL AS INFORMATION ON SHUTTLE SERVICES FROM PARKING AREAS OUTSIDE OF THE CITY. THERE IS ALSO COMMUTER RAIL ACCESS TO SALEM FROM BOSTON.

IN AUTUMN, Salem, Massachusetts, is a whole mood. Roam around any block and you'll see sweetly carved pumpkin faces and lollipop-colored mums along with plenty of skeletons, spiders, and other kinds of delightfully spooky decor filling the front yards of homes dating back to the 1600s. The city embraces a festive attitude and atmosphere unique to its historic legacy as the epicenter of the "witchcraft" hysteria in 1692. It is partly this event, which galvanized the region centuries ago and continues to fascinate today, that draws thousands to Salem each harvest season. But the aptly nicknamed "witch city" is so much more than pop culture Halloween lore or colonial-era homes. It is a diverse town with a rich arts community, an exciting, revitalized seaport scene, and a lot of beautiful scenery to inspire.

Located on Massachusetts' North Shore and resettled by European colonists in 1626, Salem seemed plagued by growing pains and struggle during the first 7 decades of white settlement. There were repeated clashes with the Naumkeag Native Americans, smallpox outbreaks, disruptive changes in colonial leadership, and even in-fighting between factions of citizens who had claimed nearby land as Salem Village. The mysterious, terrifying arrival of "witchcraft" in 1692 was enough for people to wonder, was Salem cursed? Even today, many might still ask that question.

Ultimately the Salem Witch Trials was a complicated and confounding phenomenon. Historians and sociologists have returned to this tragic, bewildering cultural event over the course of many decades to try to make sense of what happened and why. There are still no easy answers, but numerous articles and books have been published in the last decade alone that offer incredibly nuanced and thoughtful discussions about the political, religious, and cultural factors that coalesced to contribute to the rabid spread of "witchcraft" accusations.

A brief summary here: In the cold, bleak days of February 1692, 9-year-old Betty Paris and her cousin, 11-year-old Abigail Williams, began inexplicably exhibiting strange and violent behavior. Unprovoked by anything or anyone visible to the naked eye, the girls groaned and shrieked and made other incomprehensible sounds; they began crawling under furniture and contorting themselves into unusual postures; and they complained of being pinched and pricked with pins. A doctor found no physical evidence on the girls. To say that the families were concerned is a little like saying fire is hot and water is wet.

The current residents of the Emery Johnson house, ca. 1853, go all out decking their "haunted" halls for the festive fall season.

Before long other women in Salem began exhibiting similar behaviors both in their homes and at church during sermons. Betty and Abigail were intensely questioned by civic leaders. The girls accused three women—Sarah Goode, Sarah Osbourne, and an enslaved South American Indian woman named Tituba—of performing witchcraft. What followed was a living nightmare for the inhabitants of Salem and many in the surrounding settlements and townships. Accusations accelerated and snowballed. Local jails filled to the point of overflow with citizens, some of them children and expectant mothers. By May of 1692, the hysteria had reached such a frenzy and caused so much disruption that the then-governor of Massachusetts, William Phips, ordered the establishment of a Special Court of Oyer and Terminer (which translates to "to hear and determine") to prosecute cases.

The crisis reached a fever pitch in late September 1692 with the hanging of seven women and one man on a single day. Both public and private opinion was that all was turning to madness in Salem. It wasn't too long after that horrible September day that widespread support for the court began to wane. Fortunately, the governor stepped in again in October to dissolve the court,

Located at 310 Essex Street, just steps from Salem's city center, the Corwin House is the only existing structure with a direct connection to the witch trials.

A cheery garden-grown gang greets guests.

marking the beginning of the end of the witch trials. By May of 1693, Phips had officially pardoned and released anyone who remained jailed on witchcraft charges. When this chapter of Salem's history came to an uneasy close, more than 200 people had been accused with 30 found guilty and 20 of those individuals put to death. Even though the people of Salem tried to return to some semblance of "normal" life, the trauma was done and the effects of the trials would reverberate for generations.

What does this mean for contemporary Salem? One consequence of this difficult and sobering history is finding ways to balance preserving and honoring the past with acknowledging and educating about its complicated lessons. To that effect, Salem offers numerous opportunities to gaze upon its history with clearer eyes as a way to invite discussion and encourage introspection.

The Jonathan Corwin House is one of Salem's most often visited locations precisely because of its ties to the witch trial time period. Informally known as the Witch House, the Corwin residence was built in 1675.

Corwin was *Judge* Jonathan Corwin. At age 35, Corwin became heir to one of the largest Puritan fortunes in the region, purchasing the house for his family in 1675. Unbeknownst to Judge Corwin, in less than 2 decades he was going to be a part of history when he was assigned to hear and investigate claims of "diabolical activity" in Salem and some of the surrounding areas such as nearby Danvers. Corwin was installed on the Court of Oyer and Terminer, where he was responsible for sentencing individuals to jail or death.

Aside from its chilling association with such a troubled period of history, the Corwin House is an artfully preserved piece of 17th-century New England architecture. In just about any season you visit Salem, you'll often spot people gathered along the sidewalk or posing on the front lawn before you glimpse the imposing house.

By the late 20th century, many Salem citizens felt that it was irresponsible to allow the history of the witch trials to simply fuel tourism. The ordeal had happened to real people; it had caused unimaginable pain for regular families and upended the lives of descendants. It was past time to bring more sensitivity and awareness to what the trials had cost so many.

Visitors leave tokens and offerings to honor the deceased at the Witch Trials Memorial.

On August 5, 1992, the town unveiled the Salem Witch Trials Memorial, the first public monument to mark the catastrophic events more than 300 years ago. The dedication ceremonies featured an address by author, Nobel Laureate, and Holocaust survivor Elie Wiesel, who spoke movingly about the need to remain vigilant about the dangers of fanaticism that can (and do) take hold in every century, in any type of society.

Tucked into a small courtyard on Liberty Street, the memorial is simple and powerful. Four-foot-high granite walls surround three sides of the space. Cantilevered stone benches are affixed to the walls, each one inscribed with a victim's name. Similarly, words spoken directly by the victims are inscribed in the memorial's stone threshold. In many cases, the statements leave off in mid-sentence, interrupted to evoke society's disregard and lack of empathy for oppressed and persecuted individuals. The Charter Street Burying Point, the oldest graveyard in Salem, abuts the back of the memorial, acting as a kind of silent witness to this challenging history.

The Salem Witch Memorial offers a quiet, contemplative space for reflection. It is a moving and important way to put the human price of the witch trials in perspective and, ideally, raises awareness about the need to reckon with

Stop and say hello to Samantha Stevens before she jets back to another dimension.

and respect even the most difficult chapters of any culture's story.

This is not to say that Salem is without its sense of play! From its specialty stores such as the Coven Cottage and the Black Cat Curiosity Shoppe to its psychic and tarot parlors, Salem makes the most of its occult town status. And that also includes a nod to its place in pop culture fandom. Perched on a broom, ready to give her magical nose a wiggle, the statue of Samantha Stevens of the 1960s pop TV classic, *Bewitched*, can be found on the corner of Lapin Park on Essex and Washington Streets. Dedicated in 2005 and donated by TV Land, the homage to one of television's most beloved and beguiling supernatural stars is a popular photo-op spot.

A feature of Salem that doesn't always get the star treatment is its incredible architecture. More than 4 decades of architectural styles that range from the First Period, Georgian, and Federal to Greek and Colonial Revival are all on proud, beautiful display in easily accessible residential parts of the city. One of these sits a block from the Corwin House: the stately Ropes Mansion.

The successful merchant Samuel Barnard had this house built in 1727. Following Barnard's death in 1762, the mansion was bought by Judge Nathaniel Ropes II in 1768. Unfortunately for Ropes, his time in the house was not exactly a peaceful one. Ropes served as an associate justice on the Superior Court of Judicature, known as the highest court in the colony. His time on the bench coincided with a controversy involving how judges were paid:

Opposite: Flower beds and walking paths contribute to the Ropes Garden's aura of tranquility.; Pick out something from the Ropes Mansion's charming Little Free Library and claim a sunny garden bench to page away the afternoon.; The facade of the mansion has plenty of curb appeal with its white curving fence and ornately carved posts, but the house is more than just a pretty face.

The varied architecture of the Pickering House alone tells a story all its own.

which was directly by the British crown with taxes levied on the colonists. Though Judge Ropes publicly declared he would refuse the salary, he was a known Crown loyalist. Things came to a head in March of 1774 when an irate mob descended on the house, hurling sticks, mud, and rocks at the house and demanding Ropes renounce his allegiance to the King. While all this was transpiring, Judge Ropes was very near death from smallpox. He passed away the following day, his expiration supposedly exacerbated by recent events. The Ropes Mansion passed through two unmarried sisters and then eventually to the Essex Institute (now the Peabody Essex Museum) in 1907.

Visitors might also recognize this Georgian Colonial residence as "Allison's house" from Disney's 1993 film, *Hocus Pocus*. Make sure to take the walkway on the side of the house. There you'll find an idyllic "hidden" courtyard garden, installed on the grounds in 1912. Seasonal blooms and benches make it a lovely place to perch.

Leaving the Ropes Mansion and continuing along Essex puts you at the edge of the McIntire District, which is officially designated by Broad Street (on the south), Federal Street (on the north), Flint Street (on the west), and Summer Street (on the east). This is a fantastic, tree-lined "quiet zone." It's not only an ideal area for leisurely wandering, but you'll find another historic house with a lot of "wow" factor nestled in one of its tranquil streets: the Pickering House (18 Broad Street).

The Pickering House earns the dual designation of being the oldest house in Salem and one of the only residences in America to be occupied by a single family for more than three and a half centuries. John Pickering was a carpenter from Coventry, England, who settled with his wife, Elizabeth, in Salem in 1660. Pickering built his new bride a modest two-room farmhouse on a plot of land that stretched from the McIntire District down to the Salem seaport.

Colorful curb appeal at 15 Winter Street.

What resulted from John Pickering's humble first efforts ended up being a multi-generational construction marathon. Over the next three centuries, successions of Pickering family members, which included carpenters, farmers, religious leaders, scientists, politicians, and military leaders, built and modified and expanded. Different generations made period-style contributions such as gables, Gothic peaks, raised ceilings, and the wonderfully detailed fence that surrounds the property today.

You don't have to stick to the historic district to appreciate Salem's artfully designed residences. The grid of streets surrounding the Salem Common include lots of eye-catching properties that are also close to the more touristy attractions such as the Salem Witch Museum. There are also a few B&Bs tucked within this neighborhood if you're looking for accommodations with historical style and modern conveniences.

Salem is a storied city in more ways than one. It is the birthplace, home, and source of inspiration for one of America's most famous authors: Nathaniel Hawthorne. Born in Salem in 1804, Hawthorne lived and worked in various places around New England such as Boston and Concord, Massachusetts,

The House of the Seven Gables (115 Derby Street) officially opened to public tours in 1910 and has seen over one million visitors and counting.

before eventually returning to his hometown. He and his wife, Sophia, moved around Salem quite often between 1844 and 1850. One of their residences was 18 Chestnut Street, where the Hawthornes moved to in June of 1846 shortly after the birth of their son, Julian.

For a writer like Hawthorne, inspiration lay waiting for him everywhere, including Salem. One afternoon Hawthorne was visiting his second cousin, Susannah Ingersoll, who lived in a colonial-style mansion across town on Derby Street, not far from the Salem harbor. The mansion was originally built in 1668 for a seaman named Captain John Turner. Over the course of several generations, the Turners built and modified the house to add things such as casement windows, larger parlor rooms, and raised ceilings that added several gables to the home. The Turner house eventually came into the possession of the Ingersoll family who remodeled the house again, removing many of the gables to bring it up to date with the then current Georgian style of build.

As Susannah and Nathaniel visited, she told him about the house's unique architectural history. She pointed out the beams and mortices marking the original "seven gables" of Turner's initial design. Like many writers with an ear for an interesting phrase, Hawthorne liked the way "seven gables" sounded, remarking in a letter: "The expression was new and struck me forcibly. I think I shall make something of it." The novel *The House of the Seven Gables* was published in 1851 and has endured in print and in film adaptations till today.

Another interesting home in this same area is the Daniels House Inn. Designated the oldest bed-and-breakfast in Salem, the Daniels home was built by Stephen Daniels in 1667, predating the witch trials. For more than a century, this First Period residence was home to area carpenters and shipbuilders. In the mid-1700s, Daniels's daughter married and took over the house to raise her family. The Daniels house saw its share of growing pains over the centuries—at one point it was subdivided to make two

Let time stand still within the walls of the Daniels House.

sets of apartments. Eventually the Daniels House was gradually restored over the course of the late 20th century and today its historic rooms, outfitted with authentic antiques, offer guests a singular home-away-from-home experience.

It's a short walk from the House of the Seven Gables to Derby Street, which runs parallel to Salem Harbor. Stately residences and other buildings from the 18th and 19th centuries greet you on your way to enjoy some of what the waterfront area has to offer.

There are actually four distinct wharfs that comprise Salem's harbor front. They are consolidated as part of the Salem Maritime National Historic Site, which is a 9-acre section of shoreline skirting Derby Street. Richard Derby and his son, Elias Hasket Derby, began construction of the wharf that bears their name in 1762. As the coastal area expanded to accommodate the trade and fishing industries, the other wharves were added: Hatch's Wharf (1768), Central Wharf (1791), and Tucker's Wharf (early 19th century). At one point warehouses crowded the Salem wharves. Many were up to three stories high and at least one contained Hasket Derby's counting house. Today the wharves welcome commercial and private boats, dining, and recreation.

Waiting to cast off.

It's worth the short walk out on a pretty, rocky jetty to the Derby Wharf Light Station. This boxy lighthouse has been welcoming boats to the harbor since 1871. It stands only 20 feet tall and its light, once powered with oil, is now an eco-friendly solar-powered station. Derby Wharf is a great example of a marriage between preservation and progress.

Heading back toward the city center south on Derby Street toward Pickering Wharf is one of Salem's best-kept secrets: the outdoors Punto Urban Art Museum. This incredible community initiative has turned an ordinary 3-block radius of nondescript residential city buildings into towering brick canvases of spectacular art.

El Punto or "The Point" is a neighborhood of Salem located between the area of the South River and Palmer Cove. It has roots as a prime fishing center dating back from the mid-1600s. Over the centuries, El Punto has undergone numerous shifts, including housing the Naumkeag Steam Cotton Company in 1847 and enduring "The Great Salem Fire" of 1914. An influx of Latino

Opposite: *Totem* by Ledania (@ledania), Punto Urban Art Museum, a program of North Shore Community Development Coalition; A welcome beacon through the centuries; Salem's restaurants make the most of their eclectic buildings.

and Spanish-speaking residents to El Punto in the 1950s shifted the demographic and culture once more.

In 1978 El Punto became home to the North Shore Community Development Coalition (Northshore CDC), a nonprofit dedicated to improving the lives of residents, raising awareness about cultural and economic opportunities, and enhancing the quality of life for all. One way the organization decided to pursue its aims was through the creation and sharing of art. By 2013, the Northshore CDC was in talks with several other area organizations including the City of Salem, the Point Neighborhood Association, and the Metropolitan Area Planning Council about launching an arts-based opportunity aligned with its core mission and values. Punto Urban Art Museum made its debut in 2017, featuring the work of 50 muralists. Its goals remain to dismantle socio-economic barriers, promote the connective and restorative power of art, and increase opportunities for local businesses.

You've never seen public art so vibrant and immediate as these towering installations. Currently 75 large-scale murals featuring the work of 40 global and 25 New England–based artists light up the sides of buildings and walls in a series of unassuming city blocks around Peabody and Ward Streets. Each work is tagged with plaques containing QR codes scannable with your mobile phone that contain more information on the artist and the art. In addition, Punto features rotating short-term installations that often explore or speak to various cultural, philosophical, and political themes.

With so much to see, explore, and unpack in Salem, it's easy to see why so many fall under its spell, becoming frequent visitors to experience its charm and magic in every season.

Lowell

LOWELL IS 25 MILES NORTHWEST OF BOSTON, SITUATED ON THE MERRIMACK RIVER.

TAKE A TRIP INTO THE HEART OF the American Industrial Revolution with a visit to Lowell, Massachusetts. Though Lowell lacks the urban shine of other area cities such as Portsmouth or Boston, it makes up for it in working class warmth and earnestness. Lowell has a lot to be proud of, from its mill town roots, to its cultural diversity and world-class educational institutions, to shaping a hometown literary hero, Beat poet and writer Jack Kerouac. Just underneath those old, towering mill stacks lurks a lot of urban loveliness and charm.

Unlike some other New England cities, Lowell came late to the regional party, founded in the 1820s. The swath of land northwest of Boston, positioned ideally along the 117-mile Merrimack River, was mainly farmland. The parcel came to the attention of the Boston Associates, a loosely organized group of wealthy 19th-century investors including Nathan Appleton, Abbot Lawrence, Amos Lawrence, Francis Cabot Lowell, and Patrick Tracy Jackson associated with the Boston Manufacturing Company and responsible for building a lucrative textile industry in Waltham, Massachusetts. The group of men quickly saw the potential of developing land a stone's throw from such a powerful energy source. It also didn't hurt that there was already an existing canal, the Pawtucket Canal, connecting the Concord River tributary with the Merrimack. An industrial future was always Lowell's destiny.

Of the group of men, Lowell was the most vocal and visionary about this new city becoming a new model of industry for the country. A trip to London in 1811 changed the course of Lowell's life work. Inspired and energized by the design of Britain's power looms, which were highly mechanized, Lowell realized that America was poised to benefit from this type of innovation. He took his ideas back to his cohort in the Boston Manufacturing Company, promising to help create a manufacturing system that was faster, more efficient, and far more humane than the deplorable and dangerous industry conditions in England (labor was often carried out by young children in the British mill system). Unfortunately, Francis Cabot Lowell passed away 5 years before the city was incorporated in 1823. The Boston Associates named the

Left: The textile mills and factories that made Lowell a hub of work and life for people from all over the world have been carefully preserved as living and retail spaces.
Right: Merrimack Street is full of architectural flourishes on sidewalks and vintage buildings.

town Lowell after their friend and the man whom they all considered the driving creative force behind this revolutionary undertaking.

The city of red brick and watery canals took shape over the course of the 1830s and 1840s. This would become Lowell's economic, social, and urban legacy. Its traces persist everywhere, especially in the city's central shopping and dining district bordered by Market and Merrimack Streets.

Every structure in Lowell seems to speak volumes, and the building housing the city newspaper, the *Lowell Sun*, is no exception. Sequestered in Kearney Square just a few blocks from the Market Street area, the Sun Building is an example of an early skyscraper. At just 10 stories, this hardly seems like it qualifies as a high-rise. Designed by Chicago- and Paris-trained architect Clarence Blackall between 1912 and 1914, the Sun Building reflects a style popularized during the time period. The building's 2-story base eventually culminates with a neoclassical entablature, cornice, and parapet. The iconic

A classic firehouse building preserved and renovated with care and attention breathes new life into the city's contemporary social space.

Left: A young writer named Jack Kerouac briefly worked the sports beat for the *Sun* before going on to write for a different kind of Beat entirely. Right: All aboard!

sign perched on the top gives the building a retro feel as if it actually existed in a city drawn from a Marvel comic.

Though Lowell was built as a "walking city," by the 1860s its growth meant that people needed a little more than foot power to get from their homes to work in town. By 1890, electric-powered trolleys made traveling in and around the city fast and easy for everyone. Today you can ride like a true citizen of Spindle City on one of its colorful trolleys. Trolleys are free and run between the Visitor Center (246 Market St.), Boott Cotton Mills Museum (115 John St.), and Suffolk Mill (600 Suffolk St.) Thursday through Monday.

BOOTT COTTON MILLS MUSEUM
115 John St., Lowell, MA

By the 1850s, the bulk of American cotton goods and woven textiles originated on factory floors housed in the gigantic, lumbering mill buildings that lined the banks of the Merrimack River. Cotton moved in a direct route up from the southern states, which expedited the manufacturing process. No need to wait for ships from overseas. By 1860 there were more cotton spindles in Lowell alone than in the combined 11 states that would comprise the future Confederacy. The city of Lowell hummed like one of its well-oiled spinning machines.

Mill work was hard, but for many impoverished individuals there were tremendous opportunities inside its clattering walls. Germans, French Canadians, Irish, and Italian people arrived in the city in droves eager to better themselves and, in many cases, earn money to send back home to families. Places like the Boott Cotton Mill welcomed them with open arms.

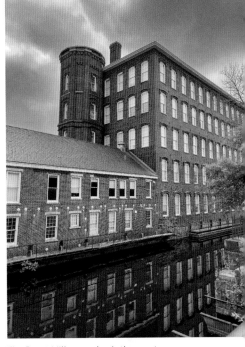

The Boott Mills complex is the most complete, preserved remainder of Lowell's 19th-century textile boom.

The Boott Cotton Mills Museum is currently under National Park Service designation. The enormous complex is part museum and part residential space and worth a visit. The mill was named after Kirk Boott, who grew up in Boston, graduated from Harvard College, and went on to study engineering in England at the Royal Military College. Upon his return, Boott found his way into the Boston Manufacturing Company in Waltham, Massachusetts. There he applied what he learned touring Britain's spinning mills. Many of Boott's sketches and notes regarding innovations and improvements to the mechanics of spinning and weaving technology would eventually be used in the factories of Lowell and other industrial city centers in New England such as Manchester, New Hampshire, and Lawrence, Massachusetts. Thanks to Boott's engineering acumen, many of these mills proved more lucrative than their British predecessors.

Boott was sent to Lowell in 1822 to act as treasurer and agent for the Boston Manufacturing Company. The group had formed the Merrimack Manufacturing Company to oversee and run its mill operations. The company prospered and thrived thanks to Boott's stewardship, and the city grew due to many of his savvy business decisions. For instance, Boott brokered a position with the proprietors of Locks and Canals, a company that controlled canal

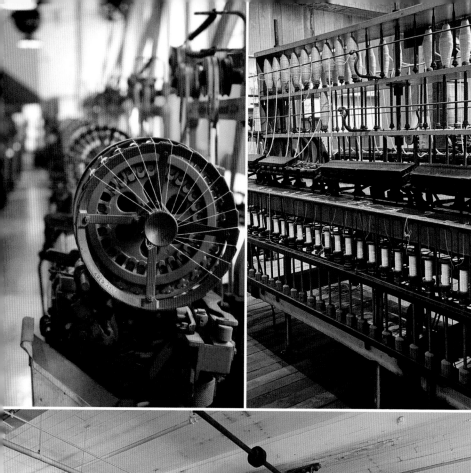
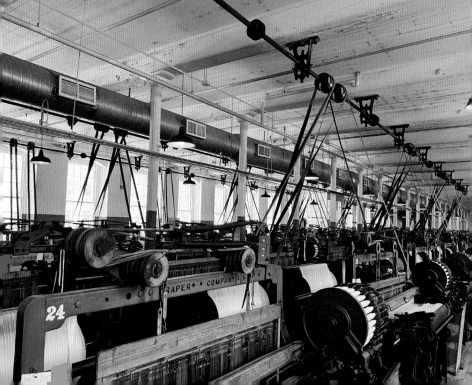

water and land. He used his influence as agent of that firm to sell unused power, which allowed other firms and factories to operate from Lowell.

Boott was intimately involved in the civic side of Lowell. He contributed to the designing of school districts, was moderator of the first town meeting, and on more than one occasion was chosen to represent the town's interests in the state legislature. Boott was also well acquainted with the people and families he employed and intimately involved in

Punch in to start your tour just like one of Lowell's many mill workers.

the day-to-day operations of the mills, including the one that bears his name to this day.

A visit to the Boott Cotton Mills Museum is a little like spending a day walking the footsteps of Boott and the hundreds of men and women who labored at weaving and spinning machines 6 days a week. The Boott affords an eye-opening look at life, labor, and technology from more than a century ago.

Along with advances in weaving and spinning machinery, the "Lowell system" of mill work was responsible for another kind of dramatic shift: employing women. Prior to this period, most industrial work was essentially subcontracted so that individuals labored in home. A place like the Boott Mill and others around Lowell housed all the spinning, weaving, and gathering under one roof. The need for onsite labor was immense. Women provided a perfect solution.

Factory managers recruited the informally known "mill girls" from area farms. Typically single, these women were between the ages of 15 and 35, paid in cash, and required to live in company-owned dormitories or rooming houses. This also helped create a safer living environment for women. Group homes were run by older women known as "matrons" who also provided meals, light housekeeping, and laundry service. A short walk from

---

Opposite: A typical mill shift lasted between 12 and 14 hours with half a day on Saturday and Sunday off.; Machines like this one at the Boott gave rise to Lowell being known as the Spindle City.; The Weave Room contains over 80 working looms from the 1920s.

---

the Boott Mill brings you to one of the surviving boardinghouses from the early 20th century.

Mill girls were also expected to adhere to a set of moral social codes that included attending religious services and taking educational classes. Hiring women made excellent business sense on several levels: Many women came with some skill and experience in weaving and spinning, and they could be paid less than men (the more things change, the more they stay the same as the saying goes). Though the work could be unbearably physically tough, many women thrived in the mills. A short documentary film exhibit on the second floor of the Boott Mills Museum captures the stories of women who worked in the mills during the 20th century. Several talked about how the mills afforded them both an economic opportunity and a sense of purpose. Most importantly for these women, mill work gave them a community.

Mill work began to wane in the years surrounding the First World War. A number of factors including the move to cheaper overseas factories contributed to the steady decline of this approach to industry. By 1958 the Boott Cotton Mill ceased operations and closed its factory doors. The building, along with many other abandoned mill sites, fell into disrepair until major refurbishment and preservation efforts began in the 1980s. Fortunately, the success of this initiative means that future generations will be able to access a connection to New England's working past as well as to hear from the individuals who lived it every single day.

LOWELL CEMETERY
77 Knapp Ave., Lowell, MA

A city's green spaces give it texture, visual variety, and much-needed opportunities to connect with nature. When it comes to creating organic spots to perch or play, there really are very few rules. And maybe that's why so many people find themselves drawn to the beautiful, tranquil surrounds of the Lowell Cemetery.

Spending the afternoon "enjoying" time in the cemetery may seem a little strange (or even suspect) to modern individuals. But in the early decades of the 19th century, this was not only a perfectly acceptable way to while away an afternoon, it was often the preferred use of someone's limited time. The American public parks movement would not gain traction until the mid to late decades of the 1800s. Many cities were overcrowded, dusty, and noisy. Lowell was no exception. Remember, the banks of the Merrimack River were

The Lowell Cemetery welcomes all.

taken up with all the infrastructure of the mill system. Where could people go for a little green escape?

The answer in 1841 was the newly created Lowell Cemetery. The "garden cemetery" trend popularized in Europe was beginning to make its way to American cities and towns. The Pere Lachaise Cemetery in Paris opened in 1804 and became one of the primary models for "rural cemeteries" in Europe and across the Atlantic. The Lachaise approach migrated the burial ground away from church property and incorporated the principles of landscape architecture to build what felt like a beautiful English garden that also happened to house plots for the deceased. A group of prominent Lowell citizens were inspired by this trend and put forth plans to build their own, more modest, form of Lachaise.

Designed by civil engineer George P. Worcester, the Lowell Cemetery featured wide, winding pathways perfect for foot or carriage traffic. It occupies 84 acres, just outside Lowell's downtown, bordered on the west side by the Concord River. The cemetery is lush with diverse tree varieties and cultivated flowering bushes; it is a lovely spot for birding and it boasts some of the most inventive "funerary art" you'll find in New England.

Take a walk along Barker Avenue to see the magnificent final resting place of Dr. James Cook Ayer, a 19th-century patent medicine tycoon.

King of the jungle keeps peaceful watch.

A truly "novel" grave marker.

Ayer was born and raised in Massachusetts, settling in Lowell where he ran his successful pharmaceutical factory until his death in 1878. His monument was created out of Italian marble in London by the sculptor Price Joy. The formidable, but sweetly melancholy, jungle cat rests atop a series of blocks forming a pedestal. Ayer's monument is stunning in its design and Joy's sophisticated and thoughtful craftsmanship gives the hulking beast the appearance and demeanor of a forlorn house pet missing her master.

Just a couple of streets over on the Maple pathway you'll find a tribute to make any book lover's heart skip a beat. The 19th-century Baker-Brandt family commissioned this 6-foot-tall granite book sculpture to celebrate and honor the clan's passion for knowledge. An inscription of a John Greenleaf Whittier poem graces the inside of the open tome.

There are more wonders to uncover scattered throughout the Lowell Cemetery. It is a welcome, surprisingly quaint oasis to slip to when you need a breather from the busy city or simply want to enjoy feeling amazed at the ingenuity of art, nature, and commemoration.

JACK KEROUAC GRAVE
Edson Cemetery
1375 Gorham St., Lowell, MA

Every fall Lowell comes alive in inspired literary spirit to celebrate one of its beloved hometown legendary artists: Jack Kerouac. The Kerouac Festival takes place over several days each October with readings, music, events, and more to commemorate the young writer born to humble beginnings in Lowell but fated to change the world of literature forever. If you can't make it to the fest, you can always plan a stop at Kerouac's grave in Edson Cemetery to say hello and pay your respects.

Born and raised in Lowell, Kerouac showed himself to be a gifted athlete in high school, which earned him scholarship offers to several renowned area colleges. He eventually entered Columbia University where he played football, but a broken leg cut his athletic career short. Not long after, Kerouac dropped out of Columbia but stayed in New York, a city that would prove indelibly influential on the young future poet and writer. It was there that Kerouac formed lasting friendships with the people who would shape him creatively and personally: Allen Ginsberg, William S. Burroughs, and Neal Cassady among others.

Kerouac's indelible words live on in his many works that remain just as fascinating and confounding as they did at the time of writing.

His checkered life—serving in the Merchant Marines, run-ins with the law—forged a lot of the energy and inspiration behind Kerouac's early writing. Kerouac's first novel, *Town and the City*, was published in 1950 and established him as an intriguing new literary voice. But it was the release of *On the Road* in 1957 that shot Kerouac to fame and cemented his place as a revolutionary figure in a circle of artists transforming the styles of novels and poetry known as the Beats.

Throughout his young life Kerouac continued to publish and push the form of his writing further and further. Unfortunately, his struggles with alcoholism ultimately resulted in his untimely death on October 20, 1969, at the tragically young age of 47. What Kerouac leaves behind, however, is a rich legacy of art and imagination as well as the enduring inspiration that anyone, from anywhere, can change the world at any time.

As a city known for being a place of constant evolution and reinvention, Lowell feels like it's just getting started. Between its emerging arts scene, its novel approach to repurposing the past, and its eclectic array of dining and recreation, Lowell is one of those places that continues to surprise you. The city's next chapter is waiting to be written. Will you add a verse?

Early morning arrives in the serene Rockport harbor.

CATCH SOME OCEAN VIEWS:
Seacoast Towns

ROCKPORT, MA

GLOUCESTER, MA

PLUM ISLAND AND NEWBURYPORT, MA

MARBLEHEAD, MA

PORTSMOUTH, NH

Rockport

ROCKPORT IS LOCATED ON THE NEW ENGLAND SEACOAST ABOUT 40 MILES NORTHEAST OF BOSTON AT THE TIP OF THE CAPE ANN PENINSULA.

ROCKPORT, MASSACHUSETTS, tends to sit in the shadow of larger seacoast cities such as Gloucester and nearby Ipswich, but its quiet, peaceful, quaint atmosphere makes Rockport an ideal place to escape to for a few hours or even a few days.

Rockport sits on the tip of Cape Ann, a rocky peninsula explored by Europeans as early as 1606. In 1623, British colonists arrived with the Dorchester Company, a commercial outfit aimed at bringing colonists to North America and providing safe haven and supplies. The area's proximity to the ocean made it the perfect location to establish fishing channels. Colonists also found that timber was in abundance and put their efforts toward harvesting the surrounding forests for wood for shipbuilding. As the area became slightly more populated with settlers, the town of Rockport grew out of the land surrounding the Cape Ann peninsula.

In the 1800s Rockport became the main supplier of the region's granite reserves. The nearby Halibut State Park contains traces of the quarries mined for vital building materials in towns and cities all over the East Coast. In fact, the demand for Rockport granite was so high, especially during America's Industrial Revolution, that a specific type of sloop was built to transport the rock.

Gradually the demand for granite decreased. Concrete and other building materials that were cheaper to acquire and transport became more widely used beginning in the 1930s. However, by this time Rockport was beginning to earn a reputation as a thriving place for artists to work and live.

Artists such as Winslow Homer, Edward Hopper, and Childe Hassam made Rockport their home during the 19th and 20th centuries. On a visit to Rockport during this time period you might find any one of these influential

---

Opposite: Cozy seaside cottages waiting for their seasonal guests; Colorful wooden buoys dot the sides of this grand seaside barn.; Motif #1 is the most frequently painted structure in America.

Little rowboats gathered in thoughtful conversation.

artists out on the wild, rocky bluffs of the town's shoreline, working at their easels in the popular "plein air" or "open air" approach to painting. Many of these painters created work in Rockport that contributed to the movement of American impressionism. This tradition continues to the present day. Artists' studios and galleries dot areas of Main Street up through Bearskin Neck, the town's main thoroughfare. This scenic quarter-mile stretch is lined with shops and delicious foodie spots. Be sure to walk to the end to venture out on the scenic rocky jetty affording spectacular views of the ocean and greater Rockport.

In keeping with its reputation for stoking inspiration, Rockport has somehow managed to transform its working harbor into an art scene all its own. Motif #1, Rockport's most famous fishing shack, is a standout feature that draws casual visitors and the creatively inclined alike.

Built in the 1840s to house fishing gear, Motif #1 appealed to the sensibilities of various painters visiting the area at the time, making it a favorite subject for brush, pencil, or camera. The original structure was destroyed in the blizzard of 1978, but the replica that stands today was quickly constructed in the same year. Everyone gets to feel like Winslow Homer or Mark Rothko when it comes to Motif #1. You can carefully walk around its perimeter to catch different glimpses of the harbor and its colorful boats as well as enjoy the Motif's cheerful, sea-themed details.

While you're there, take some time to take in the harbor itself, an unexpectedly delightful attraction with its cluster of colorful boats and dreamy reflections captured in the water from land and above.

As a coastal town, Rockport makes the most of its summer season. Free outdoor concerts and other public performances, Fourth of July festivities, and more make the hot New England summer pass like a breeze around Rockport. But don't let that stop you from checking out what this little hamlet has to offer year-round. The winter months are just as lovely for enjoying the scenery with a mug of hot cocoa or picking up that last-minute one-of-a-kind gift on your list. No matter when you stop by, you'll quickly discover why Rockport has been charming its guests for centuries and counting.

Gloucester

GLOUCESTER, MASSACHUSETTS, IS A COASTAL CITY LOCATED ON MASSACHUSETTS' NORTH SHORE, NEAR CAPE ANN.

GLOUCESTER IS AWASH IN New England shipbuilding and fishing history. It's a proud and vibrant community that carries on the legacy of generations of immigrants and others who have made Gloucester one of the country's oldest and most robust fishing ports. Gloucester is full of unexpected finds that hold a lot of fascinating cultural and artistic history, a stretch of seacoast pocketed with enclaves ripe for exploration and fun discovery.

About 20 years after the Cape Ann area was resettled, colonists formally incorporated Gloucester in 1642. Unlike other New England coastal towns, Gloucester built up its town center and primary green 2 miles inland from the harbor, though the seacoast real estate would play a vital role in the city's economic and cultural growth. Gloucester eventually grew into a critical shipbuilding and fishing community. With its proximity to Georges Bank and other marine-rich pockets of ocean not far from Novia Scotia and Newfoundland, Gloucester fishermen commanded these waters throughout much of the 19th and 20th centuries. One of America's most famous seafood businesses began in Gloucester in 1849 and is operating today: Gorton's of Gloucester featured the iconic "Gorton's Fisherman" on its products along with its catchy slogan, "Trust the Gorton's Fisherman."

By the late 1800s Gloucester had attracted scores of Italian and Portuguese immigrants to its docksides in search of more opportunity. The contributions of these communities fundamentally changed Gloucester's social, art, political, and economic makeup. Gloucester hosts several Italian and Portuguese festivals throughout the year, celebrating and upholding the heritage of its diverse citizens. One of its most well-known feasts is St. Peter's Fiesta. The past and present relatives of Gloucester's fishing community lead a procession carrying oars to represent the many fishing vessels that have resided in Gloucester's harbor over the centuries.

However, boating and fishing are not the only draws to this busy coastal community. Gloucester was once home to a man who quietly revolutionized the world one radio-controlled device at a time. And what else would fit a man who ruled the science of radio waves but a castle.

From commercial vessels to private sailing crafts, Gloucester is a boaters' paradise.

HAMMOND CASTLE MUSEUM
80 Hesperus Ave., Gloucester, MA

John Hays Hammond Jr. was only 10 years old when he set his eyes upon his first castle. Born in San Francisco in 1888, John and his family moved frequently for his father's job as a mining engineer with Cecil Rhodes in South Africa. A decade later the family relocated to England where John got his earliest glimpses of the history, culture, and design that would influence him for the rest of his life. Two years later, John had another life-changing occurrence when he accompanied his father on a business trip to West Orange, New Jersey, to meet with Thomas Edison. An inexhaustibly curious young boy, John peppered Edison with question after question, prompting the inventor to give the boy a personal tour of his facilities. Edison assumed an informal mentor role in John's life, remaining in contact until Edison's death in 1931.

These formative experiences steered the trajectory of John's life as a scientist, inventor, and art collector. He went on to attend the Sheffield Scientific School at Yale University, becoming fascinated with the relatively new study of radio waves. Another prominent figure took John under his tutelage and also remained a friend and mentor for life: Alexander Graham Bell.

When John graduated Yale in 1910 he decided to take a page out of Edison's playbook and applied for a job at the US Patent Office. Edison had demonstrated to John that inventing for invention's sake was a wonderful and worthy pursuit, but it would only take one so far. Innovation and economics went hand-in-hand, especially if someone wanted career longevity. Working in the patents office gave John an opportunity to research which nascent fields were considered financially "hot." Combining these insights with his background in radio wave science, John eventually founded the Hammond Radio Research Laboratory on land already connected to his father's estate in Gloucester, Massachusetts.

With his intellectual and life's work underway, John turned his attention to creating a residence as original and inventive as John himself. He purchased property a mile south from his father's compound and engaged the services of the Boston architectural firm of Allen and Collins in 1923 to begin construction on a tower house style. As the property and building evolved from 1926 to 1929, the residence would come to resemble the medieval castle manor it is today.

John drew upon the vast array of structures, art, and artifacts he had seen on his many world travels. Perhaps calling up that early memory of standing before one of England's many elegant and imposing castles, John knew he wanted the overall look and feel to follow in that medieval style, but he also wanted to integrate elements, materials, and artifacts from his own swiftly expanding collection of classical antiques and other items dating back to the 16th century. The result is a spectacular amalgamation of art pieces, old-world craftsmanship, and, of course, John's flare for the inventive harmoniously woven into a property that was part home, part laboratory for John and his wife, the artist Irene Fenton. From the moment you cross the threshold, visitors have a sense of moving through time without ever leaving the house.

The Great Hall is a showstopping kind of space. Unsurprisingly, it is one of the first rooms guests encounter. One can only imagine what John and Irene's frequent guests to the castle thought of its stone walls, vaulted ceilings, and arched windows and doorways during the Hammonds' tenure.

Opposite: Of course every castle needs a drawbridge! Guests begin tours of the house by passing through this regal entrance.; Standing in the Great Hall feels like taking center stage in a scene from a medieval movie or TV show. Walt Disney hosted an exclusive screening of *Fantasia* in the Great Hall.; Gaze out on the ocean through elegant stone arches in the front courtyard.

Though much of John's collection is priceless, he built his surroundings to be thoroughly enjoyed.

As if the Great Hall weren't impressive enough on its own merits, John installed a feature to rival almost every other in his castle: one of the largest pipe organs in the world. The organ was built over the course of a decade by a host of the world's most famous and skilled organ builders. John also made sure the builders incorporated 19 of his own patents in the instrument's technology. Unfortunately for John, he was unable to play the grand organ. This didn't stop his love for and enjoyment of the piece and its music. In true John Hays Hammond Jr. fashion, the clever inventor built his own device within the console that allowed the organ's music to be recorded and replayed. Visitors to the castle were usually treated to hearing the organ, and many of the world's most accomplished organists received personal invitations to play.

Another incredible centerpiece of John and Irene's home is the courtyard, which John had designed to replicate a medieval village. He utilized his collection of 15th-century facades to outfit the space, giving the sense of being both inside and outside. Each section

A vigilant friend keeps watch over a small courtyard garden.

When the Hammonds occupied the castle, it was always part residence and part working space for John and his inexhaustible imagination.

gestures toward different aspects of typical medieval life such as tavern and trade culture.

John also had builders include tropical plantings, which required a certain amount of temperature and humidity control. The 8-foot-deep pool provided the right level of moisture, while steam pipes in the bottom of the pool controlled the water temperature as well as helped regulate the moisture in the air. John not only employed all his ingenuity to his inventions and designs, he also used his staggering intellect for great fun. When the pool was created John had green dye added to complement the tropical atmosphere of the perimeter. It also helped obscure the pool's depth. One of his favorite stunts to amuse and shock guests involved taking a running start from the Great Hall, leaping upon the ancient Roman sarcophagus as a "dive board," and, to the initial terror of his guests, launching himself into the pool.

John became known as "The Father of Radio Control" for his extensive work on electronic remote control technology. His work is the reason for nearly all of our modern radio remote control devices. From the lab in his castle (current visitors can tour his Invention Room), John developed hundreds of domestic and foreign patents. He worked closely with the American government during both world wars making significant contributions related to missile guidance systems and unmanned combat aerial vehicles that aided combat efforts.

Leave enough time in your visit to explore the grounds, which offer as many fantastic, hidden discoveries as the castle itself.

STACY ESPLANADE AND FISHERMAN'S MEMORIAL
Stacy Boulevard, Gloucester, MA

A short drive from Hammond Castle Museum lies the sprawling Stacy Esplanade. This scenic prom-

Lose track of time and gain peace of mind on the Stacy Esplanade.

enade overlooks Gloucester Harbor. It is named after George O. Stacy, a prominent 19th-century real estate developer and hotelier from Gloucester. Stacy helped build up the tourist trade in the city by owning and operating several summer "cottages" (what we would now characterize as hotels) and the Wedding Cake House, an impressive Colonial Revival house built for Stacy and his wife. Mrs. Stacy disliked the house's remote location. Instead, the couple turned it into a rental property and today it is part of the Bass Rocks Inn.

The Stacy Esplanade honors Stacy's legacy as a purely recreational space. It's a wonderful place to stroll, relax, or enjoy gazing out on a pristine ocean vista.

Another feature of the esplanade is the moving tribute to the fishermen and women lost to sea known as the Fisherman's Memorial. Boston-based sculptor Leonard F. Craske created the memorial, installed and dedicated in 1925. Craske modeled his figure after Captain Clayton Morrissey, a well-known Gloucester fisherman who was also a captain of the scientific research schooner the *Effie M. Morrissey*. The stone is purposefully rough as Craske wanted to convey the rough and rugged nature of the dangerous

THEY THAT GO
DOWN TO THE SEA
IN SHIPS
1623 - 1923

fishing industry. Similarly, the captain faces the water and grips the wheel as if heading into a storm or other treacherous territory. The panel on the base of the memorial is etched with the inscription: "They That Go Down To The Sea In Ships 1623–1923."

EASTERN POINT LIGHTHOUSE

You could easily make an entire vacation out of visiting New England's many lighthouses. Check one off your lists with a visit to the Eastern Point Lighthouse.

To get to the lighthouse follow GPS directions as it takes you through a private neighborhood development. You will see signs marked "private" and "no entry," but those do not pertain to accessing the lighthouse. There is a very small parking lot, which is managed by the Massachusetts Audubon Society as the Eastern Point Wildlife Sanctuary. Mass. Audubon members can park for free; nonmembers are charged a $10 fee, payable by an envelope/collection station.

Trading with China, India, and Europe had made many Gloucester sea captains wealthy individuals. But their financial pursuits were not without great risk. Citizens began petitioning for a lighthouse as early as 1821. Local and federal bureaucracy slowed the process down until 1829 when congressional support for the lighthouse ultimately broke a stalemate between the town and President Andrew Jackson who, it was speculated, was nursing a grudge against Gloucester for not supporting his bid for the presidency. This just shows that it may bode well to have friends in high places, but not if you make them into enemies.

Lighthouse construction got underway in 1831, initially costing $2,579. Prior to this, the citizens of Gloucester had used an existing structure as a makeshift marker to help guide boats into the harbor, which was converted into a lighthouse with the addition of a wrought-iron lantern and copper dome atop a 30-foot tower. The Eastern Point Lighthouse began shining its welcoming beacon on New Year's Day of 1832. Samuel Wonson was the lighthouse's first keeper. He and his wife, Lydia, occupied the small, brick keeper's house that consisted of a kitchen and two rooms on the ground floor with additional, cozy rooms just above. Wonson was paid an annual salary of $400 for his service.

A time capsule rests in the statue's granite base containing items from 1923 when the piece was created and before it was officially installed.

The keeper's quarters built in 1879 in the Gothic Revival style stands today. Winslow Homer, the famous American artist, spent much of 1880 painting views and scenes of the lighthouse and its surroundings.

Though the citizens of Gloucester were pleased to finally have something resembling a proper homing beacon on their shores, which were often the site of difficult and damaging landings due to the makeup of its natural coastline, this Eastern Point Lighthouse was not without its drawbacks. The lantern room was considered quite small with its 6-foot diameter. Any keeper attempting to trim the wicks of its 10 lamps, fueled by whale oil, would not be able to stand comfortably or safely. The local engineer I. W. P. Lewis inspected the lighthouse in 1843 and cited several serious violations: The light itself was perilously decayed, leaky, lacked proper ventilation, and was in dire need of rebuilding. Lewis conceded that the lighthouse's location was essential and it should not be moved or torn down; rather he advised reducing the number of lamps to one to ensure its effectiveness as well as to address the problems he had already identified.

Wonson added a few more of his own observations and notes to Lewis's report, which would eventually find its way to Congress. He wrote that the lighthouse tower itself leaked "in every direction"; ice covered the walls during the winter and horrid green mold in the humid summer months; the windows were loose and the casements rotting; and every storm that blew with gale force winds in every season threatened to break the lighthouse's glass. Fortunately, Congress took the report seriously and approved funds to tear down and rebuild the lighthouse in 1848.

The new Eastern Point Lighthouse became active on November 3, 1848, rising 30 feet high to welcome boats safely with its fixed white light.

The light from Eastern Point remained steadfast over the next century while change and innovation took place. For instance, a new fourth-order Fresnel lens installed in 1857 significantly increased the lighthouse's visibility from 11 to 13 miles. Between 1894 and 1905 a 2,250-foot-long breakwater was created in the front of the lighthouse over an area of dangerous reef known as Dog Bar Reef to better protect the harbor. More than 200,000 tons of granite blocks from nearby Cape Ann were used to construct the barrier. A small wooden tripod featuring a light rested at the end of the breakwater to deter ships from crashing into it, giving lighthouse keepers the additional task of caring for the "mini" beacon known as Dog Bar Breakwater. Electricity made its way to the station in 1896 with telephone service implemented the following year. The lighthouse keepers had never before enjoyed such modern conveniences. By 1985 the lighthouse became fully automated. The city held a ceremony and Carroll Wonson, the great-grandson of Samuel Wonson, the lighthouse's inaugural keeper, was given the honor of being the final person to manually turn on the light.

Today the Eastern Point Lighthouse is operated and maintained by the US Coast Guard. Direct access to the lighthouse quarters is prohibited. The grounds are intimate, but there is still plenty to enjoy picking your way around the coastal frontage. It's a wonderful spot to explore tidal pools and relax by the water with a light snack. A walk out on Dog Bar Breakwater allows you to take in the quietly regal Eastern Point Lighthouse from the same vantage point as countless sailors did centuries ago.

BEAUPORT, THE SLEEPER-MCCANN HOUSE
75 Eastern Point Blvd., Gloucester, MA

Hammond Castle Museum is not the only real estate marvel in Gloucester. Along the coast on the same stretch of road that takes you to Eastern Point Lighthouse sits what at first appears to be just another modern, coastal mansion. A closer look reveals a house plucked from the pages of a fairy tale inside and out. This is the design and architectural marvel of Beauport, the Sleeper-McCann House.

Built in 1907, the Sleeper-McCann House is a marvel of interior design elements and materials culled from all over the world and keenly presented by Henry Davis Sleeper.

Henry Davis Sleeper was only 28 when he first traveled from Boston to the beautiful, wild seacoast enclave of Gloucester in 1906. By this time, Gloucester and its surrounding communities such as Rockport had earned a reputation as a seaside getaway for wealthy, affluent, and artistically eclectic New Englanders. Isabella Stewart Gardner, whom Henry would come to know as a dear friend and creative co-conspirator, spent many carefree summer days picnicking, boating, and attending parties in Gloucester. Though it's unclear if Henry ever received any formal education, he was making a name for himself in the growing field of interior design. Prior to the late 19th and early 20th centuries, a home's interior design might have been instinctively put together as part of the overall building process. The rise of wealthy families building and buying lavish properties shifted this approach to one that was more careful, thoughtful, and often curated based on the individual's personal tastes. Architects began hiring artisans specifically to cultivate the look, atmosphere, and presentation of these spaces. That's where a person like Henry Davis Sleeper would come in and the result, especially in Henry's hands, was often pure magic.

While living in Boston Henry had become friends with A. Piatt Andrew, an assistant professor of economics at Harvard. Piatt had built his own summer mansion in Gloucester, named Red Roof, and invited Henry as his guest. Henry instantly fell for the breathtaking coastal views, the luxurious tranquility, as well as for Piatt's smart, interesting, wonderfully inventive group of bohemian friends that, in addition to Isabella, included the painter Cecilia Beaux, the intellectual Joanna Davidge, and Caroline Sinker, a renowned New England patron of the arts.

A year later Henry purchased land a short distance from Piatt's Red Roof and began construction on the residence he referred to as Beauport—a name that harkens back to the phrase "Le Beauport" or "beautiful harbor," which was first used by explorer Samuel de Champlain when he arrived in

Pick a book and curl up in any number of Beauport's magnificent nooks and crannies.

Gloucester in 1606. What began as a modest Arts and Crafts–style house featuring the signature elements of wide, open floor plans, gabled roofs, and exposed beams steadily grew along with Henry's voracious appetite for antiques and art collecting. Eventually, the 40-room house would showcase a range of architectural periods from Gothic and medieval to early colonial.

It's not just the stunning, dizzying architecture that makes Beauport so special; much of the allure lies in the way Henry went about staging and outfitting every space. Henry was a passionate enthusiast for repurposing and salvaging materials and artifacts. For instance, he incorporated pine paneling from an 18th-century home in Essex, Massachusetts, that was about to be sold and demolished. He took endlessly novel approaches in consistently bringing together the marriage of design and function such as in creating a display for his collection of amber glass.

Henry installed an artful leaded-glass door he salvaged from a Connecticut home as a grand display case. A skylight in the pantry just behind the door filters in natural light to make the luminous collection perpetually back-lit. Henry replicated this effect elsewhere throughout the house with purple, green, and red colored pieces of glass.

Natural light makes Henry's
130-piece amber glass
collection glow with warmth
on even the gloomiest of
New England days.

Though Henry attended to most of the house's rotating design pieces and evolving elements, he relied on architect Halfdan M. Hanson for his building needs. Hanson emigrated to Gloucester from Norway when he was an infant. After completing education in Philadelphia, Halfdan spent the bulk of his life living in Gloucester and building many iconic properties around the area. He formed a close personal and professional relationship with Henry that lasted over 27 years. The pair collaborated well. Halfdan seemed to understand the nature of Henry's genius and would often construct an entire room based

Guests dine at the edge of the world at Beauport.

solely on a singular element Henry acquired. This was the case with Beauport's circular tower library.

Halfdan constructed the room around the panes of glass that Henry obtained from a glass-enclosed hearse in England. The softly gathered drapes are another one of Henry's playful winks: They are made of wood.

In other spaces Henry liked to express his flare for the dramatic. The "Golden Step" room looks directly out onto the limitless ocean. It is named after the *Golden Step* sailing vessel and is also an homage to Gloucester's maritime legacy. Henry was also known for mixing his own paint colors, resulting in one-of-a-kind hues such as the ethereal shade of seafoam green that dominates the room's color scheme.

The view isn't the only "wow" factor waiting to surprise guests gathering in the "Golden Step." Henry had the diamond-shaped windows outfitted with a pulley system hidden underneath the floor. In summer months or in warm weather the windows could be lowered completely for a spectacular alfresco dining experience.

Henry's reputation for interior design seemed to expand along with the storied walls of Beauport. His client roster would eventually include his good friend Isabella as well as Henry Francis du Pont and Hollywood legend

The wallpaper came from a Massachusetts home built in the 1780s belonging to Robert Morris, a signer of the Declaration of Independence. The paper depicts aspects of Chinese trade industries.

Joan Crawford. Throughout his career he would use Beauport as an informal showroom, meeting clients at the house. Even so, everything Henry collected and purchased for his home had personal value—it brought him joy or delight or he found the artifact fascinating or simply wonderful.

Sadly, Henry's life was cut short due to leukemia. He remained a bachelor when he passed away in 1934. Henry's brother inherited Beauport, but he could not afford the upkeep. Fortunately, the property came to the attention of the preservation-minded Helena Woolworth McCann in 1935. McCann was the heiress to the Woolworth department store fortune. She kept the house largely intact with all of Henry's treasured items while adding pieces from her own collection of art and antiques. She used Henry's lavish "China Trade" room as her primary space for entertaining guests. One of the only changes she made to the space was removing a massive, authentic Chinese pagoda that dominated one wall and adding a brilliant Waterford crystal chandelier.

Every room in Beauport is a showpiece. Thanks to Henry's indelible creative zeal, each space hums with life, heart, and a deep appreciation for the simple wonder contained in everyday objects—if you are willing to look a little closer. You could easily tour the home every week and find something new, which is part of the joy of visiting. And though Beauport contains many precious, priceless items, it radiates with Henry's warmth in every lovely nook and cranny.

ROCKY NECK ART COLONY
Parking lot on Rocky Neck Avenue, Gloucester, MA

For more than a century, artists have flocked to the New England seacoast to soak up its inspiration along with its ocean air. This particular stretch of regional coastline has attracted its share of painters, photographers, sketch artists, and more. Today you can witness that legacy in action with a tour through Gloucester's Rocky Neck Art Colony.

The peaceful neighborhood of Rocky Neck is home to the area's oldest continuously operating art collectives. Eclectic galleries and studio spaces fall along a short stretch of Rocky Neck Avenue, making it an easy place to discover a range of styles, approaches, and mediums. Whether you're

Come to support working artists, but stay to soak up the whimsical atmosphere of Rocky Neck Art Colony.

shopping, appreciating, or mining inspiration for your own canvas, Rocky Neck Art Colony promises something fresh and original with every visit.

Forged by the same challenging elements that carved its shoreline, Gloucester is a city that knows it has a lot to offer sea- and land-lovers alike. As a primary source of the nation's seafood supply, Gloucester's enduring fishing community is a model of resilience and New England ingenuity. With such a rich variety of areas to explore and facets to discover, there seems to be about as many ways to partake in Gloucester's rich culture as there are seafaring stories about "the one that got away."

Plum Island and Newburyport

NEWBURYPORT IS A COASTAL TOWN LOCATED 35 MILES NORTH OF BOSTON. IT ALSO CONTAINS THE PLUM ISLAND WILDLIFE REFUGE.

Lovely blooms signal the beginnings of spring on Plum Island.

PLUM ISLAND

A renowned wildlife refuge, Sunset Drive Beach, and trail access can be found at the Parker River National Wildlife Refuge on Sunset Drive. A gatehouse marks the refuge entrance where you can pay to access any of the seven different parking lots. From wherever you decide to start, it's a short amble to the nearest trail or walking path.

Slip into a seaside nature preserve of reedy marshes, sandy dunes, and cool stands of pine and cedar forests with a trip to Plum Island, Massachusetts. Plum Island draws upon both fresh and salt water environments: bordered on the north by the mouth of the Merrimack River and the Ipswich River to the south with the Atlantic Ocean on the east. As a result, visitors get to experience a range of rich ecosystems and wildlife in this 11-mile stretch of preserved land.

Named after the variety of plum shrubs that populate the sandy dunes, Plum Island was once used by early colonists in the nearby towns of Ipswich, Rowley, and Newbury as pasture land for cattle, hogs, and horses. Like so much of New England transformed during the Revolutionary War, this modest piece of land was also drawn into conflict. Fort Philip was built on the northern point of Plum Island in 1776 to defend it against potential attacks along the Merrimack River. The fort was used again later in the War of 1812, but had completely eroded and disappeared by the 1830s.

Over 350 species of birds call Plum Island home, making it one of the region's most popular birding destinations.

The biggest conflict you'll find on Plum Island today is deciding where to stake out the perfect birding spot. It is a beloved and busy place for spying many avian marvels. All season long people can catch sight of countless species, from snowy owls and red-breasted nuthatches in the fall and winter months to bobolinks, bald eagles, warblers, indigo buntings, and more during the warmer season. And that's only what you'll find with your eyes to the skies. Also known as "the great marsh," the swampy, grassy flats teem with egrets, ducks, and great cormorants.

And each spring the island gets a visit from a VIP guest: the piping plover. These wee 7-inch-long shorebirds are currently on the Endangered Species List. Thanks to a massive

Pack some snacks, put air in the bike tires, and enjoy a tranquil afternoon making your own island discoveries.

conservation effort begun in the mid-1980s, Massachusetts has led the way to increasing the population and providing ongoing protection for these charming, feathered ocean friends. Every spring they migrate to beaches and lay three to four sandy-colored eggs that both male and female plovers incubate for about 27 days. Their size makes them an easy casualty of busy beach foot traffic. Refuge conservation staff close areas of Plum Island trails and beaches during these crucial times to allow the plovers to "pipe" their little ones in peace and safety.

Well-maintained walking trails take you through sandy outcrops, forested sections, and stretches of pristine beach. The main road through the island is paved making it safe for cars and bikes. However you choose to get around on the island, you will want to do it leisurely and with frequent stops so you don't miss a thing.

When you're ready to shake the sand from your shoes and refuel with a lobster roll or latte, make the short 7-mile trip from Plum Island to downtown Newburyport. What is now a major shopping and foodie locale was a thriving maritime center in the early 1700s. From manufacturing clipper and whaling

Spend time admiring water views along the tranquil wharf.

ships in the 1800s to prospering in the fishing industry to currently hosting one of only 19 surf stations for the US Coast Guard in the country, Newburyport preserves and celebrates its role in shaping New England seacoast history. You can get a sense of this by walking along the wharf just steps from the downtown shopping district. Markers designate significant milestones in the town's nautical past: The point known as Tracy's Wharf was a base for American privateers and British prizes captured during the Revolutionary War, while Warehouse Point was the first wharf built in 1655 by Captain Paul White.

Finish up your stroll and head back toward Merrimac Street, which runs parallel to the harbor. From there you can easily spend time shopping and nibbling up and down State Street and the surrounding grid of streets. One of the coolest aspects of Newburyport is uncovering its offbeat, funky character with eateries like The Grog, a city dining destination for over 40 years, and indie, boutique shops such as Dyno Records.

Newburyport has worked hard to preserve its colonial heritage. By the 1950s and 1960s, much of the city had fallen into extreme disrepair and economic crisis. There was even talk of razing the entire downtown historic district and rebuilding. Thankfully, cooler heads prevailed and city officials obtained a federal grant to keep much of its historic architecture as well as allot funds

Opposite: Keeping it real and classic since 1976, Dyno sells vinyl and used CDs, as well as turntables and musician gear like capos and tuners.; Some art just has to live in the wild.; A pint of "grog" of your choice awaits at this popular Newburyport eatery.

Stately homes once belonging to sea captains and their families pay tribute to the city's past.

toward the preservation and upkeep of various properties. Finely restored residences dating from the 18th and 19th centuries remain centerpieces of the quiet, tree-lined streets bordering the downtown shopping district.

Over the last several decades, Newburyport has earned a reputation as an up-and-coming arts hub. Independent galleries along with the Newbury Arts Association are housed along Water Street, a few short blocks from downtown.

While you're in that area, the Tannery Marketplace is worth stopping by. In the mid-1980s, a series of tannery buildings were bought and environmentally sanitized to become a multipurpose complex. In addition to retail, the site hosts summer and winter farmers' markets as well as live music and other arts/culture functions.

There's no need to rush your time in Newburyport and there's no shortage of ways to experience all it has to offer. An afternoon spent reading by the wharf, an early morning bike ride along the harbor rail trail, a meet for coffee at an outdoor cafe, or a paddle along the Plum Island marshes are all fantastic Newburyport experiences. Follow the pull of your own personal tide to enjoy all this charming seaside city has to offer.

Pick up some fresh blooms to sweeten the ride home at the Beach Plum Flower Shop located in the Tannery Marketplace.

Marblehead

MARBLEHEAD SITS ON A SMALL PENINSULA EXTENDING INTO THE NORTHERN PART OF MASSACHUSETTS BAY.

MARBLEHEAD IS ANOTHER COLONIAL-ERA New England town that has had a front seat to history. Marblehead shipyards supplied the first naval vessels for the Revolutionary War. The *Hannah* was the first vessel commissioned for the army, outfitted with state-of-the-art cannons and a stalwart crew from Marblehead. A large number of men left the town to fight in the war, specifically on ships engaged in battle at sea and within New England's besieged waterways. At least one of these crews was instrumental in aiding the Continental Army's escape during the Battle of Long Island in 1776. And it was men from this quaint seacoast town who ferried General George Washington across the Delaware River for his attack on Trenton in

Opposite: The Old Town House decked out in patriotic bunting to welcome seasonal visitors from around the world; Below: A series of colorful colonials dating from the 1700s line State Street.

Window box whimsy.

the same year. Many historians and scholars cite these contributions as evidence that Marblehead was the birthplace of the American navy. Throughout each successive American military conflict—the War of 1812 and the Civil War—the citizens of Marblehead consistently served and sacrificed. During the Civil War Marblehead was not only the first regiment in the state to answer the call for troops, but those who remained on the home front raised nearly $100,000 to supplement the war effort, an astonishing accomplishment and moving gesture from a town with such a small population and simple means.

Traces of Marblehead's legacy remain nearly everywhere from the colorful, Georgian- and Federal-style houses lining its streets to the grounds of Fort Sewall Park, to the sleepy inner harbor that helped make Marblehead a successful fishing port in the early 1800s. You can easily take in all this history and more by meandering through the streets encircling Marblehead's town center.

In addition to lovely boutiques and specialty shops, you'll find buildings such as the Old Town House, the city's first town hall. Built in 1727, it also served as a forum for heated debate during the American Revolution where people such as Elbridge Gerry and General John Glover spoke passionately about liberty and freedom from British rule. Nearby is another property with ties to revolutionary foment. The Robert "King" Hooper mansion, built in 1728, housed Federalist meetings in the decades leading up to war.

Washington Street comprises the town's primary shopping and dining neighborhood and will also lead you to some of Marblehead's beautiful green spaces and harbor inlets. Follow Washington to Orne Street and detour up the short hill to the Old Burial Hill Cemetery. Established in 1683, the cemetery is laid out along gently rolling hills, trees, and peaceful views of the harbor and ocean beyond. It also contains a small pond dotted with benches, perfect for pausing to enjoy some reflection and refreshment.

FORT SEWALL

Access Fort Sewall by going to the end of Front Street. There is a very small parking lot at the bottom of a short incline that leads you to the entrance of the fort grounds.

Another beautiful and moving spot to visit in Marblehead is Fort Sewall on Gale's Head, the northeastern point of Marblehead's peninsula. It was fortified as Gale's Head Fort in 1634 and characterized as one of the oldest English fortifications in the United States. From the Revolutionary War to the start of the War of 1812, the fort was rebuilt and expanded. Additions included a blockhouse and an increase in munitions.

It was during the War of 1812 that the fort saw some of its most spectacular and heroic action. On April 3, 1814, the British frigates HMS *Tenedos* and HMS *Endymion* essentially cornered the USS *Constitution* in the shelter of the fort. The fort was no match for the warships, lacking the munitions to defeat or at least drive off the warships. Instead the fort pulled the kind of bluff you might see in a blockbuster Hollywood movie, running out its guns in a bluff as if they were preparing to attack. Met with a 44-gun frigate and the seemingly massive defensive powers of a fort, the British captains voted to retreat, not realizing they had been played. Not long after, the fort received the name that

The site of historical turmoil has now become a place of tranquility.

persists today: Fort Sewall, after Samuel Sewall, a chief justice of the Massachusetts Supreme Court from 1800 until his death in 1814.

Fort Sewall weathered the last of its military conflicts during the Civil War and the Spanish-American War of 1898. By 1892 the town had voted to adopt the fort as a park and later, in 1922, transferred ownership to the federal government.

Paved walkways ring the property, and plenty of benches invite visitors to rest and relax while enjoying views of Marblehead's sleepy harbor.

MARBLEHEAD LIGHT AT CHANDLER HOVEY PARK

Also known as Lighthouse Point, Marblehead Light is located at the end of Follett Street. The GPS for Chandler Hovey Park will direct you to the correct location.

To experience another side of this peaceful coastal destination, head across the harbor to Chandler Covey Park and Marblehead Light Station. The word *lighthouse* conjures images of a white tower adorned by a powerful searchlight. Marblehead Light bucks that trend with its 100-foot-tall, pyramidal structure made of iron.

There are only about 14 of these types of pyramidal skeletal lighthouses in the United States and Marblehead Light is one. In 1884 the Lighthouse Board

A lighthouse unlike any other in New England to complement a not-your-average coastal town.

standardized the building plans for these kinds of skeletal lighthouses, stipulating they measure 100 feet in height with a square footprint. The Sanibel Island Light Station in Florida was the first to adopt these updated mandates. Marblehead Light followed when it was built in 1896.

The lighthouse is perched atop a rocky rise on the point of a 3.74-acre parcel of land known as Chandler Hovey Park. The land was originally owned by the federal government before resident Chandler Hovey purchased it in 1948. He gifted it to the town as a green space open to the public. Though Marblehead Light is architecturally distinct, it's really Hovey Park that delivers a bit of a "wow" factor. Rocky outcroppings for climbing mingle with sprawling green spaces perfect for picnicking. Benches punctuate the gently sloped terrain, positioned to showcase the picturesque harbor along with its friendly fleet of boats and Marblehead raising its lovely face in the distance.

Even in the busy summer months with tourists and residents hitting beaches and taking to the waterways up and down the coast, Marblehead somehow manages to maintain a homey, unhurried atmosphere. Marblehead might just be New England's best-kept secret for an easy, relaxing, low-key day trip with all the benefits of a long weekend getaway.

Spend time in this little patch of seaside paradise.

Portsmouth

PORTSMOUTH SITS ACROSS THE PISCATAQUA RIVER, BORDERING MAINE.

PORTSMOUTH, NEW HAMPSHIRE, IS THE "little black dress" of New England seacoast towns: versatile for every type of travel taste and classically enduring through the centuries. Perched on the Piscataqua River, a coastal tributary that forms a natural ocean harbor, Portsmouth is a seamless blend of natural and urban spaces. Catch a whale watching or sunset cruise; discover the downtown artisan shopping scene; or gather supplies for a lawn lunch and head to one of the city's lovely green spaces. There are so many ways to experience this charming town you'll be hard pressed to pick your favorite.

By the early 1600s European explorers had found their way to the area that would eventually become Portsmouth. The first mention of the territory came in a report by Martin Pring, an English explorer who led several expeditions to scout for viable land and settlement places in the "new world." Two decades later British captain and explorer John Mason capitalized on Pring's

Locally owned independent shops, cafes, and other retail destinations line bustling Market Street.

The facades of Portsmouth eateries are a feast for the eyes.

efforts. Mason lived in the town of Portsmouth in England's Southampton and carved out a bit of a checkered life for himself that included piracy and run-ins with the authorities. The feverish "land rush" gripping Britain at the time meant many companies were purchasing lands in new territories outside of the continent and establishing colonies and plantations. Mason became involved with at least one of these groups, which eventually led him to set his sights on the area of "the new world" described by Pring.

Mason teamed up with fellow English military commander, Ferdinando Gorges, to apply for a massive land grant from the Plymouth Council of New England for "all the territory lying between the Merrimack (NH) and Kennebec (Maine) rivers." Ambitious, greedy, or maybe both, the council awarded Mason and Gorges their request in 1629 with the provision that the land be split along the Piscataqua River. Mason received control over the southern half. Mason's new colony was rechartered as the Province of New Hampshire and it included most of what is currently the southeastern part of present-day New Hampshire as well as parts of modern-day Massachusetts north of the Merrimack. Ironically, Mason never got the opportunity to travel to New England and see his newly acquired land for himself. He was appointed vice

The North Church's beautiful facade and iconic steeple cuts an impressive sight at the top of Market Street.

admiral of New England in 1635, but passed away during preparations to make the journey.

When the colony became a proper township in 1653, it was named Portsmouth after Mason's hometown in England. With its ideal placement along the river and with access to the Atlantic corridor, Portsmouth quickly established itself as an important seaport for trade, fishing, shipbuilding, and in later decades, military conflict. During the American Revolution, for instance, Portsmouth was a critical access point for French ships transporting vital munitions, supplies, and other goods to aid the colonial militia. Similarly, the Portsmouth Naval Shipyard was established in 1800 as the first federal navy yard. It gained notoriety in 1905 as the site of the signing of the Treaty of Portsmouth, which ended the Russo-Japanese War.

Today, the echo of those earlier shipbuilding and seafaring centuries resonates throughout the city, especially in the downtown shopping and dining district with its rows of colorful storefronts and red brick facades. The grid of streets that make up its primary shopping district—Market, Hanover, Bow, State, and Islington Streets—is a great place to spend time exploring and getting to know this highly walkable city.

Specialty shops and boutiques, sweet cafes, fine and casual dining, art galleries, and funky concert venues make the area so much more than a shopping district. Thanks to Portsmouth's longstanding artisan culture, the city's historical character has been preserved alongside tasteful and playful modern development. A short amble up Market Street brings the spectacular North Church into view.

The North Church has been a fixture of Portsmouth since the 1700s. President George Washington attended service in one of its first incarnations in 1789. Over the course of the centuries, the church has undergone various renovations, upgrades, and even rebuilds due to fire or other types of damage. The North Church that currently exists dates back to 1854 with one of the most recent, extensive renovation and preservation efforts occurring in 1978. The North Church has always been affiliated with Protestantism and remains an active place of worship. Currently, the church is affiliated with the United Church of Christ, a progressive Protestant denomination that aims to provide conscientious, inclusive worship and fellowship to all.

Pieces of the city's past are scattered everywhere. From the Moffat-Ladd House (tucked on a quiet end of Market Street), once home to William Whipple, one of America's Founding Fathers and signers of the Declaration of

Independence, to the 19th-century Portsmouth Music Hall that hosts all types of live performance, there is heritage on every corner. For a deeper dive into Portsmouth's New England roots, a tour through the city's Strawbery Banke section is a must.

STRAWBERY BANKE

The Strawbery Banke Museum is located at 14 Hancock St., but the neighborhood itself encompasses a 10-acre area of streets characterized as an "outdoor history museum" an individual can walk and explore at their own pace.

One of the first British colonials to begin reclaiming land in the Native American territories along the Piscataqua was a military officer and explorer named Captain Walter Neal. He took land along the river, constructed a settlement, and named it "Strawbery Banke," presumably for the thick patches of wild strawberries spread along the shoreline. Gradually a neighborhood formed, informally called Puddle Dock for its proximity to the nearby tidal inlet.

People maintained their residences in the area for centuries, enduring the shifts, changes, and growth of the city around them. However, in the 1950s,

The sunny Tobias Lear House on Gardner Street, built in 1750 for Tobias Lear, a merchant and ship's captain whose son, also named Tobias, served as private secretary to President Washington. The house operates as a museum, open to the public.

city officials designated the entire area a candidate for "urban renewal," which meant razing, rebuilding, redeveloping, and essentially erasing a huge part of Portsmouth's history. Fortunately, several civic groups and other concerned individuals had been paying close attention to these developments. They turned their alarm into action, forming Strawbery Banke, Inc. in 1958. Their efforts, along with the contributions of many others, helped save and preserve Strawbery Banke. They created a museum space as well as worked to preserve more than 30 buildings made available to the public for tours and programs.

Waiting to catch the tide.

You can visit the museum and tour several properties, but you can also make your way through the idyllic little neighborhood to discover these houses with their unique charm at your own pace. Point your feet toward Court Street—head west, away from the harbor. Within a couple of blocks you'll start to see the first of these historic houses. Most are designated with plaques and all boast distinctive architectural styles that range from colonial through Georgian and Federal styles. You will think you rounded a corner and happened upon a movie set.

Just around every turn in this narrow warren of streets you'll find eye-catching decor and wonderful details on these centuries-old residences. As most are private homes, always be respectful when you're taking photos or admiring the architecture or details closely (and keep an eye out for cars making their way down these narrow streets). Wind your way down Gardner, Pickering, or Hunking Streets to arrive alongside the sleepy end of the harbor that empties into a quiet marina. This stretch is a great "hidden gem" for admiring the waterfront without a ton of crowds. It also puts you on the road over to Prescott Park and nearby Peirce Island, two of the town's most prized green spaces.

Colorful houses built along the city's oldest
historical section, Strawbery Banke.

PEIRCE ISLAND AND PRESCOTT PARK (105 MARCY ST., PORTSMOUTH, NH)

A scenic walk over Peirce Island Bridge (just off Mechanic Street) takes you to a beautiful 27-acre island, which doubles as its own kind of floating city park. Here you'll find paths that skirt along tidal pools and rocky outcroppings as well as marshy inlets and plenty of green spaces and benches for pressing pause. The remains of two historic forts are also on Peirce Island: Fort Washington (named after George Washington) and Fort Sullivan (named after a local war hero, John Sullivan), both constructed in 1775. There are a few short hiking loops as well as plenty of places made for ocean gazing.

You can leave the wilds of Peirce Island behind and head back toward town along Mechanic Street to pass through Prescott Park, Portsmouth's artfully designed and wonderfully welcoming park and performance space.

Known for its fantastic outdoor summer concert and theater series, Prescott Park runs along the water on a parcel of land purchased in the 1930s by two sisters: Josie and Sarah Prescott. The sisters were public school teachers and passionate about their beloved city. In the 1930s, they quietly began using funds from an inheritance to purchase properties along the river, including one that was vastly run down and derelict. The Prescott sisters saw potential in the space for their ultimate dream: building a scenic waterfront park and pavilion for the public to enjoy. After the sisters passed in 1954, they willed the land to the city for public use.

The Prescott sisters' legacy remains in the form of a beautifully maintained 10-acre public park that includes several formally designed garden beds, installed and maintained seasonally by city staff, and a thriving summer theater and performance series (the Prescott Park Arts Festival). Whether posing for pics on the boardwalk by the water or surrounded by a patch of lush roses or lounging with a book and blanket underneath one of the park's trusty oaks, you will find Prescott Park is one of Portsmouth's loveliest and most tranquil locations.

For a relatively small town, Portsmouth is packed with delightful finds seemingly everywhere you look. One of those is simply too big to miss: the World War I Memorial Bridge (also referred to as Memorial Bridge). The original bridge was constructed between 1920 and 1923. Like so many types of American infrastructure, the Memorial Bridge experienced steady wear and tear over the decades. By the turn of the 21st century, it was also showing signs of being mechanically outdated—as recently as 2009, officials were forced to

The Formal Garden includes seasonal blooms as well as benches to relax and take in this sweet natural oasis in the midst of a busy town.

lower the weight restrictions of vehicles crossing from 20 tons to 10, significantly hampering traffic and busy supply routes. In 2010 city, state, and federal officials approved the budget to replace the bridge, which reopened in 2013.

A walk over the new Memorial Bridge is another fun way to see a completely different side of Portsmouth. It also gives you travel bragging rights: Where else can you visit two states on foot in less time than it takes to eat an ice cream? Memorial Bridge spans the Piscataqua, connecting Portsmouth with Badger's Island, in Kittery, Maine.

Badger's Island was also a thriving shipbuilding community in the 19th century; many of the earliest ships of the US Navy were built in the shipyards of this small town. There are a few places to grab a bite as you come off the bridge, but really it's the waterfront scene that is worth the short interstate trip. As you cross over, look out for the Buoy Shack, a hole-in-the-harbor seafood restaurant. More than a place to get your lobster roll fix, the shack is a charming, quirky photo-op spot. Vibrant, colorful buoys hang on the small shack, which gazes out at "the big city" across the river.

With Portsmouth you'll get a dose of big-city energy delivered in a homey, small-town atmosphere. Add to this the seamless incorporation of stunning natural locations and it's clear that if there is such a thing as a town "having it all," Portsmouth fits the bill.

Does it get any more quintessential
New England seacoast than this?

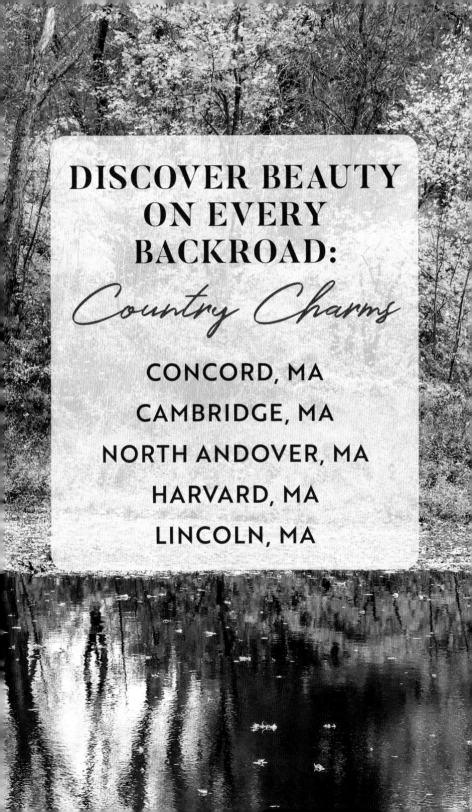

DISCOVER BEAUTY ON EVERY BACKROAD:

Country Charms

CONCORD, MA

CAMBRIDGE, MA

NORTH ANDOVER, MA

HARVARD, MA

LINCOLN, MA

Concord

CONCORD IS A MIDSIZE TOWN LOCATED ABOUT 24 MILES NORTHWEST OF BOSTON.

A PROSPEROUS, BUCOLIC SUBURB of Boston and home to a host of American literary luminaries, Concord, Massachusetts, might be considered one of New England's most storied towns.

Concord was originally known as "Musketaquid," the Algonquian term for "grassy plain" in reference to the low-lying marshes and kettle ponds. Anyone's first glance could see there was a lot to love about this wild, unspoiled area: huge expanses of rolling fields, thick stands of forests, and the Assabet and Sudbury waterways teeming with a ready food source. English colonists pounced on the rural curb appeal. Two British men spearheaded the resettlement of Concord in 1635. Reverend Peter Bulkeley and Major Simon Willard won a land grant from England's General Court. They took a group of fellow English citizens to the Musketaquid land and "negotiated" a deal for the parcel with the local Native American tribes.

Until that fateful April day in 1775, the residents of Concord lived relatively peaceably as farmers, tradespeople, and clergymen. The proximity of Concord to Boston, the center of intellectualism, arts and sciences, and political debate, made the town a rich incubator for thinkers and writers. Fortunately for contemporary visitors, Concord has worked hard to preserve its literary legacy through the preservation and upkeep of the homes and place where many of these larger-than-life men and women of letters lived and created.

LOUISA MAY ALCOTT'S ORCHARD HOUSE
399 Lexington Rd., Concord, MA

A stop at the Louisa May Alcott Orchard House is like spending time with the famed characters of Alcott's most celebrated work, *Little Women*. In addition to the main house, the property contains the smaller building that Amos Bronson Alcott, Louisa's father, used for the Concord School of Philosophy, which operated from 1879 to 1888. Both the sweetly curated grounds and the expertly restored and maintained structures make the Alcott residence a special place to visit.

Louisa May Alcott and her family took up residence at the Orchard House in the spring of 1858. The family had moved 21 times in 30 years, mostly due

Constructed in 1857 by Amos Bronson Alcott, Louisa May's father, the Orchard House sits on 12 acres of land and has had few structural changes since its build.

to financial circumstances. Louisa's father was an educator and intellectual who subscribed to the philosophy of transcendentalism—a set of philosophical and spiritual beliefs about the inherent goodness in man and nature. He went on to found an experimental school that incorporated this framework into its pedagogy. During Louisa's young life the family experienced a great degree of instability and upheaval, which many scholars and historians credit for shaping Louisa's supple imagination and stoking her passion for writing.

Due to the intellectual and social circles Bronson moved in, Louisa and her siblings were exposed early on to tremendous figures who became dear family friends such as Ralph Waldo Emerson, Nathaniel Hawthorne, Margaret Fuller, Julia Ward Howe, and Henry David Thoreau. These individuals encouraged Louisa in her literary pursuits; they also gave her an important sense of community and belonging.

To help support her family, Louisa worked as a teacher, seamstress, governess, and writer. Lucky for readers, it was writing that stole most of Louisa's attention. She published her first book in 1849. *Flower Fables* was a collection of tales written for Ralph Waldo Emerson's daughter, Ella. She began publishing more prolifically as an adult. Between 1863 and 1872 Louisa anonymously released more than 30 gothic thrillers, popular reading of the time period. It would be the *Little Women* series, which began with part one, *Little Women or Meg, Jo, Beth, and Amy*, put out by Robert Brothers publishers in 1868, that earned Louisa an enduring place in American literary history.

The story is a partly autobiographical account of Louisa's own childhood and experiences with her siblings growing up in Concord. She based the heroine, Jo, on herself and drew inspiration and sketches from other real figures and happenings in her life. Readers and critics alike fell for *Little Women* and Louisa's life would change forever from the success.

Louisa remained active in women's rights as well as in literary circles until she passed away from a stroke in 1888 at the age of 55. Generations of readers continue to find their way to Louisa's books and stories to this day. Her words will always inspire, but it's the way she lived with quiet, steadfast resilience and a commitment to her values that resonates centuries after her last chapter ended.

RALPH WALDO EMERSON HOUSE
28 Cambridge Turnpike, Concord, MA

After departing the Orchard House, consider calling on one of Louisa's famous literary pals with a visit to the Ralph Waldo Emerson House.

An educator, essayist, intellectual, philosopher, and spiritual leader, Emerson's most "radical" ideas about the nature of man and, well, nature began to take shape at a young age. After spending some time following college teaching and working as a pastor, Emerson traveled to England. There he met and formed great friendships with several of the leading writers and intellectuals of the time such as William Wordsworth and Samuel Taylor Coleridge. These men influenced Emerson's philosophical thinking to the point that when he returned to America in 1833, Emerson threw himself into the popular lecture circuit. He made his speaking debut in Boston on November 5, 1833, in the first of what would grow to become 1,500 lectures. The topic: "The Uses of Natural History." Much of this work would find its way into Emerson's first widely published essay, "Nature."

When Emerson returned from his European trip, he settled in Concord. By this time he had been widowed, but was courting a woman named Lydia Jackson who lived in Plymouth, Massachusetts, a coastal town south of Boston. Emerson had no interest in relocating, leaving behind the rambling fields and inspired ponds and rivers of

Ralph Waldo Emerson and his family lived in this warm "sylvan" home for more than 40 years.

his beloved Concord for the "muddy" city streets of Plymouth. In July of 1835 Emerson purchased a house and land known as the Coolidge Castle property, originally built in 1828 as a summer residence for the wealthy Coolidge family from Boston.

Emerson set to work developing and revitalizing the grounds. In a letter to his brother, William, Emerson remarked that his new land was "in a mean place and cannot be fine until trees and flowers give it a character of its own." Determined to bring his surroundings in alignment with his philosophical and spiritual beliefs, Emerson spent years cultivating the lush and vibrant landscape that exists today.

The house became Emerson's creative and social sanctuary. He lived there for the remainder of his life, penning many of the iconic, groundbreaking essays such as "The American Scholar" and "Self-Reliance" from inside its warm, welcoming walls.

The body of Emerson's work and his contributions to literature, culture, philosophy, and politics are immense. From his role as one of the founders of transcendentalism to his support for abolition during the Civil War and his vast volume of essays and lectures, Emerson's fingerprints can be found on many of our contemporary ideas and movements, and we are better off for it.

WALDEN POND STATE RESERVATION
915 Walden St., Concord, MA

While we're making the rounds of Concord's prominent wordsmiths, it's a good idea to check in on one of the town's gentle literary giants: Henry David Thoreau.

Thoreau was a chronic stroller. On any given day you might find him roaming 6 or 7 miles around Concord and its surrounding forests and rivers. In his lifetime, Thoreau made epic treks such as one where he traversed 30 miles along the coast of Cape Cod. He believed walking enriched your observations and sharpened your mind. Thoreau wrote: "Moreover, you must walk like a camel, which is said to be the only beast which ruminates when walking." The steps did wonders for Thoreau emotionally, intellectually, and creatively. Over the course of his life he published several books of poetry and produced volumes of essays, articles, and journals.

Thoreau was born and raised in Concord, a place that brought him a great deal of peace and joy as well as inexhaustible curiosity. He earned a degree

"I went to the woods because I wished to live deliberately," wrote Thoreau in his introduction to *Walden*.

from Harvard College, studying rhetoric, science, math, and philosophy. When he returned from school in 1837, he accepted a teaching appointment, but resigned early on after refusing to use corporal punishments on his students. This type of value system would seed itself in everything Thoreau did, beginning with a life-changing incident in July of 1846.

Concord's tax collector, Sam Staples, sought out Thoreau and charged him with 6 years of delinquent poll taxes. Thoreau refused. He wanted no part of what, in his opinion, the government was funding such as the Mexican-American War and slavery. Staples had no choice but to jail Thoreau. The next day a "helpful" relative paid Thoreau's bail, even though it was expressly against his wishes. The entire experience stayed with the young man from Concord. He gathered his thoughts into a lecture he delivered in February of 1848. It was well received by influential individuals such as Bronson Alcott and his new friend and mentor, Ralph Waldo Emerson. Thoreau revised the essay, titling it "Resistance to Civil Government" (later it became known as "Civil Disobedience") and published it in the widely read *Aesthetic Papers* in May 1849.

Thoreau's political, social, and philosophical sensibilities aligned him with Emerson and other transcendentalists. A year prior to his arrest, Thoreau was already in the midst of an experience that would deeply impact his thinking and worldview. Without school or a dedicated job, Thoreau felt restless. His good friend, fellow transcendentalist and poet Ellery Channing, suggested Thoreau build himself a shelter along the shores of nearby Walden Pond, a beautiful, sequestered glacial pond set against a wide perimeter of woods. In the spring of 1845, 27-year-old Thoreau felled trees, planed the wood, and assembled a one-room structure for himself.

The site of the structure remains today. Visitors can access Thoreau's dwelling by following a marked trail that arcs around Walden Pond, which is also a popular swimming and boating destination. The site was excavated and officially marked in 1945. Roland Wells Robbins, an avocational archaeologist, dug for 3 months to eventually unearth remnants that disclosed the exact site of the house. From as early as the late 1800s, visitors happening upon Thoreau's dwelling continued a practice of leaving stones to pay homage to the gentle soul who devoted his life to the keen observation and appreciation of nature.

Thoreau lived at Walden for 2 years. He subsisted off fish and a plant-based diet of crops he was able to grow. His days passed tending to his "land," swimming, boating, reading, and, most importantly, taking copious notes on just about everything. He extensively recorded all aspects of this natural habitat from wildlife and plant species to the changes of ice depth on the pond in winter. Out of this intense personal and naturalistic sojourn, Thoreau compiled a series of 18 essays into the book, *Walden or Life in the Woods*, published in 1854. *Walden* was only casually received in Thoreau's lifetime, but it has become an enduring, revered work today.

Thoreau continued to travel extensively—on foot, by canoe—around New England over the course of his short life. He became a land surveyor and highly sought after amateur botanist. Thoreau also continued to publish and was in the midst of revising what would become the books *The Main Woods* and *Excursions* when he died from complications from tuberculosis in 1862. Thoreau was only 44.

Traces of Concord's beloved writers are found throughout the town, and you can pay your respects to each of them in the Sleepy Hollow Cemetery.

AUTHORS' RIDGE AT SLEEPY HOLLOW CEMETERY

Bedford Street, Concord, MA

To get to Authors' Ridge, take the Author's Gate entrance of the cemetery. If you are driving, there is a very small parking lot just inside the gate to park and explore on foot. Follow Sleepy Hollow Avenue around to the right as the cemetery gently inclines. The writers' grave markers are at the top of a ridge and can only be accessed on foot.

Established in 1855 and dedicated by Ralph Waldo Emerson, the cemetery is designed in the "garden" format prevalent in 19th-century landscape design. Head to Authors' Ridge to spend some time with these writers and think-

Guests leave tokens and offerings to Concord's sweet, poetic son.

ers who changed the world by speaking, writing, and living their truths. Here you'll find the graves of Henry David Thoreau, Louisa May Alcott, Ralph Waldo Emerson, and Nathaniel Hawthorne all within arm's length of one another.

THE OLD MANSE AND THE OLD NORTH BRIDGE

The Old Manse is located at 269 Monument St. There is ample parking just across from the site. The Old North Bridge is part of this property.

Long before Emerson, Thoreau, or Louisa May Alcott were finding their way into the nation's history books, the town of Concord had already written its own unforgettable entry.

The Old Manse is a stately residence overlooking the banks of the Concord River and Old North Bridge. The home was built in 1770 for the Reverend William Emerson, the town minister and grandfather of future transcendentalist, Ralph Waldo Emerson. Reverend Emerson resided in the spacious house nestled against fields and bordered by woods with his wife, Phebe, and their two children, William and Mary. The Emersons had settled into a peaceful life in the Massachusetts countryside when on a damp April morning of 1775 the world as they knew it changed forever. One can imagine the Emerson family gazing down from a second story window at the scene unfolding yards from the manse: on one side of the Old North Bridge, a lethal red wave of soldiers

Pure tranquility.

The Nathan Hosmer House, built in 1828, showing off its summer blooms.

dressed in scarlet coats advancing; on the other boys and young men in home-spun clothes, shouldering little more than muskets and grim determination. The fight for American independence had officially begun.

The Emersons remained in the house for generations, which included Ralph Waldo and his siblings. In later years, the Emersons rented out the Old Manse. Ralph Waldo Emerson's dear friend and fellow writer, Nathaniel Hawthorne, stayed at the house in 1842. Hawthorne was newly married to the transcendentalist Sophia Peabody, whose path had crossed with Emerson previously. Both of the Hawthornes were instantly taken with the town and enjoyed hosting many gatherings at their temporary residence attended by well-known poets and intellectuals such as Margaret Fuller and Ellery Channing. They also cherished the overall solitude and nature. This was especially beneficial to Nathaniel, who produced several short pieces during his tenure there that would eventually become the collection *Mosses from an Old Manse*, published in 1846.

The Old Manse was eventually transferred from the Emerson estate to the Trustees of Reservations around 1939 and is open for guided tours and educational programs.

There is plenty to explore on the grounds of the Old Manse such as the Old North Bridge and the Little Boathouse. A lovely way to approach the Old North Bridge is to first follow the path alongside the Old Manse down to Little Boathouse. Added to the property in 1892, this adorable boathouse squats at the end of a short dock where many boaters cast off from on any given sweet summer afternoon. The boathouse also offers a beautiful view of the Old North Bridge, often in stunning reflection when the water is still and glassy.

Peace and equanimity now pervades the grounds of the Old Manse.

The Little Boathouse is made for fishing and dreaming.

Take the trail that skirts the edge of the river over to the Old North Bridge. The original bridge was constructed in the 1650s to facilitate an easy route for farmers to get into town. Flooding and other sorts of damage to the bridge meant it typically needed replacing every 20 to 30 years. The current bridge, built in 1956 and meticulously restored in 2005, is a replica of the bridge that existed on that unforgettable April day. The Old North Bridge is part of the Minute Man National Historical Park, run by the National Park Service. Most days there is a ranger on hand to answer questions and give talks. Every April on Patriots' Day (held the third Monday of April), you can grab your own front row seat to history with reenactment events at the foot of the bridge.

Even if you are short on time, you can still experience a lot of Concord's charm with a brief tour along Main Street and the surrounding streets. Antiques shops, artisan boutiques, family-run cafes and eateries, as well as some of Concord's prettiest homes are all within a neat proximity.

It's easy to feel like you've escaped to the distant countryside with Concord's abundant wild fields, natural tributaries, and acres of wooded conservation land. It's no surprise that despite all his far and wide wanderings, Thoreau never wanted to call anywhere else home.

Cambridge and Watertown

MOUNT AUBURN CEMETERY

Main entrance at 580 Mount Auburn St., Cambridge, MA

Note: Additional entrances may be found on Coolidge Avenue and Grove Street. The cemetery can also be accessed via the MBTA Red Line: take the Harvard Square stop and walk up Brattle Street.

Part eternal resting place, part arboretum and nature preserve, Mount Auburn Cemetery is an exceptional destination. Sequestered within the busy urban centers of Cambridge and Watertown, Massachusetts, this sprawling 175-acre sanctuary is known as America's first "garden" cemetery.

The grounds include over 5,000 trees of 700 different varieties, countless flowering shrubs and blooms, several ponds and water features, and a 64-foot-tall observation tower that offers panoramic views for more than 60 miles. When people aren't paying their respects to the dearly departed, you might see them scanning the treetops with binoculars and spotting scopes. The cemetery is home to more than 80 species of birds, drawing avian enthusiasts throughout the year, in every type of seasonal climate. In fact, it's such a popular birding spot that staff keep a regularly updated chalkboard at the entrance of the main gate detailing what birds to look for.

Mount Auburn was the vision of Jacob Bigelow, a highly respected Boston physician and avid botanist. In 1815 Bigelow was appointed a professor of materia medica, a branch of medical science focused on the sources, nature, properties, and preparation of drugs, at Harvard Medical School. His medical and plant-based interests intertwined in his post and allowed him to publish extensively on plant-based benefits of floral specimens found all over New England. Given the nature of his research aims, it makes sense that Dr. Bigelow would light upon the idea for a way to inter the deceased that also incorporated the organic properties and processes of the natural world.

As early as 1825 Bigelow began formulating ideas for a "rural" cemetery similar to the peaceful, green Parisian cemetery, Pere Lachaise Cemetery. Bigelow also understood that creating such an expansive space would help

The stately, Gothic-style Bigelow Chapel, named after cemetery founder Jacob Bigelow.

Take in sweeping views of the Boston skyline from Washington Tower.

address another issue many churches and towns were experiencing at the time: The conventional practice of interring deceased individuals beneath churches often led to unsanitary conditions. With the help of the Massachusetts Horticultural Society, Bigelow's notion became a reality: The Massachusetts Legislature authorized 70 acres of land for the construction of a garden cemetery and in 1831 Mount Auburn Cemetery officially opened its gates to the living and the recently departed alike.

Bigelow was instrumental in designing the cemetery. He worked alongside Henry Alexander Scammell Dearborn, the first president of the Massachusetts Horticultural Society, and Alexander Wadsworth, an area landscape architect, on Mount Auburn's many features. The early appeal of the cemetery was immediate. It opened during that time period before cities and towns regularly implemented parks, greens, and commons as part of their civic designs. Word spread so quickly about the lovely, scenic atmosphere of Mount Auburn Cemetery that in the 1840s it was ranked alongside Niagara Falls and Mount Vernon as one of the most popular tourist stops in the country.

The cemetery is made for meandering, though a map is helpful. There's a main entrance that runs along Mount Auburn Street, which is also a moderate walk from the Harvard Square T (subway) stop. Additional entrances can

Blooms to make eternity a happily ever after.

be found on Coolidge Avenue and Grove Street. Like a friendly neighborhood, there are streets and pathways marked with signs, but there's truly no "wrong" way to access or explore the grounds. The observation tower is located around the center of the cemetery and can be approached via Walnut, Chestnut, or Magnolia Avenues.

Because the cemetery is overrun with such beautiful flora and fauna, there's something lovely to experience in every season. However, a trip to Mount Auburn in the fall produces some special natural fireworks, most notably the thread-leaf Japanese maple. Scattered throughout the grounds, at first glance these small shrub-like trees with their shaggy overcoats appear unremarkable. Duck underneath their branches and prepare to have your senses dazzled with the riot of colors thrown by their delicate leaves. Take a few minutes and marvel (and snap away!) at the way these trees seem to come to life, grooving, twisting, and dancing to the music of Jacob Bigelow's incredible dream.

Like standing inside a disco ball.

There are more than a few notable New England individuals who made Mount Auburn their final resting

Inspiring even in permanent repose.

place: philanthropist and patron of the arts Isabella Stewart Gardner; historian and Pulitzer Prize winner Arthur Schlesinger Jr; poet and abolitionist Julia Ward Howe; and the founder of the Church of Christ, Scientist, Mary Baker Eddy.

The impressive and beautiful Eddy memorial sits on a gently sloping hill overlooking the cemetery's Halcyon Lake landscape. Designed by Edgar Swartwout, Eddy's memorial is made of white granite. It features iconography significant to Eddy's work and life and eight 15-foot columns that support a coverless rim so that nothing would stand between Eddy's grave and heaven.

Numerous quiet places welcoming reflection or rest; abundant greenery, blooms, and natural elements to surround you; and stunning wildlife in every season—Mount Auburn Cemetery is an inviting place to spend a little time or all of eternity.

North Andover

STEVENS-COOLIDGE HOUSE AND GARDENS

153 Chickering Rd., North Andover, MA

When the Stevens family, one of the founding families of North Andover, Massachusetts, acquired the Ashdale Farm property in 1729, they had no way of knowing their modest, working farm would one day serve as a prized piece of natural beauty delighting future generations from all over the world. A visit to the Stevens-Coolidge House and Gardens feels like traveling to a bucolic English country estate.

Ashdale remained a farm for several generations before it fell to Helen Stevens in the early 1900s. Helen married John Gardner Coolidge, the son of one of Boston's most prominent, wealthy "Brahmin" families in 1901. John was a descendant of Thomas Jefferson and the nephew of the beloved Isabella Stewart Gardner. The couple decided to make Ashdale their summer residence. This was part of an overall trend among affluent Americans that increased in popularity between 1890 and 1930 that involved transforming their rural land holdings into seasonal retreats, often drawing inspiration from the artfully cultivated gardens of Europe.

Helen and John enlisted the services of Joseph Everett Chandler, an architect who mainly worked in the Colonial Revival style. Between 1914 and 1918, the property underwent extensive changes. Chandler modified the existing farmhouse and completely redesigned the landscape. He added perennial and rose gardens (both in keeping with the Colonial Revivalist sensibilities). He also installed a "potager garden" (a series of raised beds) that included pathways and a winding brick wall enclosure. Inside the house was decorated with Asian porcelain, American furniture, and more decorative art pieces from Europe. The fields, forests, and orchards that the Stevenses had once relied on for food and wages were culled and developed to serve as a charming pastoral backdrop for the newly created elegant agricultural estate.

John passed away in 1936 and Helen in 1962. As part of her wishes, Helen stipulated that the property that had brought so much joy to her family for generations should be made available to the public. She bequeathed Ashdale to the Trustees of Reservations, which renamed it the Stevens-Coolidge House and Gardens in honor of Helen and John.

Rows of luxurious tulips greet guests in late April and early May.

The house is open to tour during the main season (May through October) and may be intermittently closed "off-season." The grounds are always accessible and they deliver up lots of delights. Perennial blooms in the gardens create a shifting landscape. The estate's wooded borders set the scene for peaceful walks. There's always something new to enjoy on the property, including special events curated by the Trustees of Reservations group that maintains the estate—all perfect excuses to become a habitual guest and relish rediscovering what this special place has to offer.

Harvard

FRUITLANDS MUSEUM
102 Prospect Hill Rd., Harvard, MA

What first appears as another typical piece of New England farmland tells a much different story, part of a fascinating chapter in Massachusetts culture. For a precious 7 months between the fall of 1843 and winter of 1844, Amos Bronson Alcott, father of the renowned author, Louisa May Alcott, ran a self-sustaining community collective known as Fruitlands.

Alcott was an ardent transcendentalist. He embraced the philosophy behind this movement that society and its institutions corrupted an individual's purity. Transcendentalists advocated for the idea that people inhabited their highest selves when they were self-reliant, independent, and attuned to intuitive thinking. For Alcott, Fruitlands represented a potential utopic community where people could fully live these transcendentalists' beliefs and practices.

Sadly for Alcott, Fruitlands was abandoned due to poor crops that made it impossible to survive. The land was nearly lost to development until 1910 when New England philanthropist and author Clara Endicott Sears purchased the property for her summer residence. Sears restored the original farmhouse where Alcott and his family lived during their tenure at the property.

While exploring the countryside, Sears came across a small group of Shaker women in the nearby town of Harvard. The Shakers were a religious sect formed in England in the 1700s that gained acceptance in colonial America. Spiritually, Shakers believed in receiving messages from God during religious services and revivals. Culturally, they embraced egalitarian ideals with women

The farmhouse is the only original building on the property and is on the National Register of Historic Places.

The Alcotts hosted many of their like-minded friends such as Ralph Waldo Emerson and Henry David Thoreau to discuss philosophy and spiritualism.

performing spiritual leadership roles alongside men. Their lifestyle was communal, celibate, and utopian. Most notably, Shakers valued the art and practice of physical labor. They became known for their simple, well-crafted furniture, tools, and mechanical innovations. Shakers believed deeply that creating anything was in and of itself an "act of prayer" and it showed in everything they made.

Sears became close friends of the women and in 1918 when the Shaker community closed, she purchased one of its buildings, built in 1794, and had it moved board by board and reassembled on the grounds of Fruitlands.

Fruitlands encompasses five collections, referred to as "museums," first established by Sears: the original Fruitlands Farmhouse; the Shaker Museum, the first such museum in the country; the Native American Museum, celebrating the history of indigenous peoples; the Wayside Visitor Center, a classroom, education, and exhibition space; and the Art Museum. Each museum contains period art and artifacts.

Thanks to both the Alcotts and Sears, Fruitlands preserves history and culture from these diverse communities all in one place for modern travelers to discover. In addition to the museum buildings, guests can test their transcendental mettle on easy, maintained wooded hiking trails that loop through the 91-acre property. Currently maintained by the Trustees of Reservations, Fruitlands offers all types of other programming during the temperate months. Art installations, live music performances, lectures, and events like fairy house decorating fun for kids of all ages keep the original spirit of inspiration, learning, and fellowship alive in ways that would make all its founders proud.

MINUTE MAN NATIONAL HISTORICAL PARK

Visitor Center: 210 N. Great Rd., Lincoln, MA

Follow in the literal footsteps of Revolutionary-era colonists who fought for America's independence by exploring the paths that make up the Minute Man National Historical Park.

On April 18, 1775, in Boston, the British general Thomas Gage gave the order to Lieutenant Colonel Francis Smith: gather 800 men and head west toward the town of Concord. He tasked the men with seizing and destroying all munitions, provisions, and any other types of stores held by the rebellious colonists that the troops might encounter. By dawn fighting was breaking out between the soldiers and the recently formed local militia at the town of Lexington and then again at the Old North Bridge in Concord. As the sun came to rest in its noonday cradle on April 19, 1775, British soldiers had already suffered scores of casualties with more to follow. Realizing the peril he had unwittingly put himself and his men in, Gage brokered a hasty retreat. By then it was too late;

In the morning hours of April 19, the peace of these green fields used for farming was shattered by musket fire.

"Witness houses" let the walls talk, if only in whispers.

Smith's troops would never reach the safety of Boston in enough time. Thousands of colonial militia swarmed the area and engaged in musket fire. At day's end, the "battle field" was spread across 18 miles of territory that spanned the towns of Lexington, Concord, Lincoln, and Cambridge.

Today informational plaques along the Minute Man Trails tell this story and more. Over the course of several miles, you can walk under the same trees and along the same stone walls as the ordinary farmers, merchants, and proud citizens who fought to help America become a new nation.

Informational placards positioned at various places along the trails provide further details about both the conflict itself and the people living along what would become known as the "Battle Road Trail." Characterized as "witness houses," several of these structures remain, having been preserved and restored. It is impossible not to look upon the houses and imagine the scenes unfolding right in their own front yards.

One of these is the Smith House, home to Captain William Smith and his wife, Catherine, and their three young children. British soldiers passed by both to and from their march to Concord. The Smiths treated a wounded British soldier who was left behind and later expired. From the distance of our modern present, it's easy to view the past as one-dimensional, something that happened a long time ago to "someone else." A walk along the Minute Man Trails shatters that perception, bringing the real, ordinary lives of the people who experienced this terrible, extraordinary day into proximity.

As part of the National Park Service, the Minute Man park also offers educational programs, historical talks and lectures, guided tours, and periodic reenactments. The trails are well maintained and invite casual walking as well as respectful biking and exercising. It's a gift to be able to not only enjoy the grounds for their natural surroundings, but to also experience a sense of what it might have been like to take part in such a powerful chapter of America's story so many centuries ago.

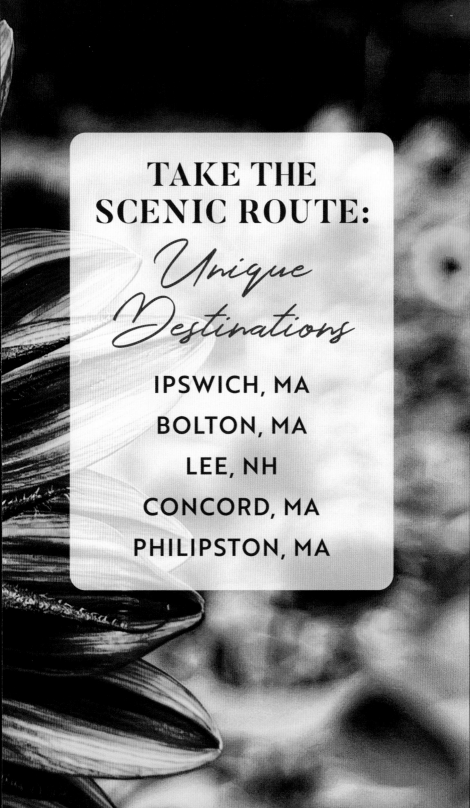

TAKE THE SCENIC ROUTE:
Unique Destinations

IPSWICH, MA

BOLTON, MA

LEE, NH

CONCORD, MA

PHILIPSTON, MA

Ipswich

THE CRANE ESTATE ON CASTLE HILL
290 Argilla Rd., Ipswich, MA

Each summer beginning in 1929, the Crane family would call this 17th-century-inspired mansion, along with its nearly 3,000 acres of woods and marsh and 7 miles of pristine beach, their home. The Crane Estate on Castle Hill offers all the grandeur of these opulent Jazz Age–era homes nestled in the bucolic New England seaside town of Ipswich, Massachusetts.

Richard T. Crane Jr. was the son of Richard Crane, a well-known Chicago businessman who had amassed a fortune manufacturing and selling bathroom fixtures and plumbing supplies just as the "indoor plumbing" craze was taking off. By the time Richard's son came into the Crane Co. business, they had significantly expanded to supplying industrial valves, elevators, and much of the pipe used for the central heating systems in the buildings of Chicago's rising skyline. By 1910 the Crane Co. owned several manufacturing plants in the Midwest and Northeast, employing more than 5,000 people and producing more than $1 million worth of goods per year.

The first several decades of the 20th century witnessed an incredible surge in the accumulated wealth of families and individuals. It was very fashionable for individuals such as the Rockefellers, Vanderbilts, and Carnegies to own seasonal residences up and down the mid-Atlantic coastline. The mansions were often simply palatial playgrounds that families occupied anywhere from a handful of weeks to a couple of months each year. The Crane Estate was no exception.

Crane purchased the land for his future estate in 1910 and began a building process that would ultimately take more than a decade to complete. He began by hiring the equivalent of landscape architect royalty to design the grounds: the Olmsted Brothers, sons of the revered Frederick Law Olmsted. Their contribution was a series of elaborate terraced gardens and the beginning of what would become the estate's "Grand Allee," a rolling half-mile lawn dotted with statuary along its perimeter. Crane dismissed the Olmsteds in 1913 and brought in Arthur Shurcliff, another

One end of the garden houses a columned balcony above a small fountain and narrow, curved pool that seems to meander like a river.

The Crane Estate waits to receive summer visitors.

Even with their wealth, the Cranes were practical people. Mrs. Crane's elegant bathroom features faux marble that is actually wood—a building material cheaper to buy, source, and transport.

well-known landscape designer to complete the property. Shurcliff improved upon the Olmsteds' efforts, finishing the allee, and also establishing two main gardens fashioned as distinct "rooms": the Italian Garden and the Rose Garden. Each featured ornate plantings, sculpted walkways, fountains, and elaborate stone work.

With the property taking shape, Crane needed a grand home to match. He hired the Boston firm of Shepley, Rutan and Coolidge to construct an Italian Renaissance–style villa. It featured stucco walls and a red tiled roof. Crane thought it was perfect. Florence Crane, his wife, did not. She found the overall design horrid and complained the house was cold and drafty and generally unpleasant. Crane compromised with his wife. He asked her to give the mansion a 10-year trial period. If she still hated it, he would replace it. She did and he did. The Italian villa was torn down in 1924.

This time Crane hired the highly sought after Chicago architect, David Adler. The result was a regal Tudor Revival–style residence with many ornate touches such as octagonal towers and inset roundels. The interior consisted of 59 rooms with similarly fine craftsmanship on display. For instance, the library features elements such as ornate wood carvings imported from Cassiobury House, an English country house razed in 1922 with many of its materials sold at auction. Other interiors also borrow materials salvaged from an 18th-century London townhouse on Dean Street. And of course, many of the most magnificent materials were saved for, where else, the Crane family bathrooms.

The Crane Estate was finally completed in 1928. Sadly, Richard Crane would only spend one summer at his property. In 1931, on his 58th birthday, he suffered a heart attack and passed away. Though the stock market crash of 1929 had not adversely affected the Cranes personally, the downturn in business meant Richard Crane had to close factories and put people out of work. Some speculated the stress and grief from putting people in more hardship hastened his death. The property eventually passed out of the family in the 1950s and, luckily, into the care and stewardship of the Trustees of Reservations, a nonprofit organization devoted to the historic preservation and land conservation of properties and natural places in the Commonwealth of Massachusetts. In addition to tours, the estate hosts weddings, special functions, public concerts, and other unique events such as the annual Roaring Twenties Lawn Party.

Walking trails dot the property that also allow beach and dune access. However, a tour of the Great House gives visitors an up close and personal glimpse into what summer life was like for the Cranes. While touring the grounds and house, let your imagination unspool. Cast yourself in the role of a Crane family member, friend, or lucky guest and envision a perfect summer afternoon of sailing and swimming followed by dining and dancing to the music of a string quartet drifting over the Grand Allee as night falls and the stars appear, seeming to shine just for you.

NASHOBA VALLEY WINERY
100 Wattaquadock Hill Rd., Bolton, MA

When you hear the phrase "wine country" you might think of rolling hills in California or Italy. Think again! The beautiful Nashoba Valley in western Massachusetts is home to Nashoba Valley Winery, New England's premier vineyard for fruit wines and more.

What began as a wine making hobby for Jack Partridge in the late 1970s grew into a rich (and delicious) family legacy that has continued for more than 40 years. Partridge spent a couple of years making wine right out of his house when he realized his pastime was becoming a full-fledged passion. He upgraded to a rental space in a mill building in West Concord called Damon

One of Jack's living contributions is the fruit produced from his experiments, with over 100 varieties of antique apples incorporated into many of the wines and ciders made today.

Mill in 1980 and began to build a business. Before much longer, Partridge set his sights on locating an orchard where he could hone his skills in harvesting different fruits for wines. Three years later he happened upon Upland Farm, an idyllic property in the country community of Bolton, Massachusetts.

Jack Partridge literally sowed the seeds of what would flourish into a place that is a little more than just a working winery. The Nashoba Valley Winery is an inviting, relaxed place where guests can socialize in a beautiful, lush natural setting. When Partridge purchased the property it also included a rustic farmhouse, built in 1923. He and his family lived in the house until Partridge sold the winery to its current owners, Rich and Cindy Pelletier. Building upon Partridge's legacy, the Pelletiers have transformed the residence into J's Restaurant.

The winery is Massachusetts' top-rated fruit wine producer as well as a pioneer in the "winery orchard" space. The team's savvy innovations and thoughtful expansions mean there is always something unique (and delicious) to experience with every visit.

Nashoba Valley Winery is a great off-the-beaten-path type of destination that raises the level of New England agrobusiness. The winery and its gathering spaces knit together the laid-back sensibilities of West Coast culture with the breathtaking landscape of the East Coast region to treat visitors to the best of both worlds.

SUNFLOWER FESTIVAL AT COPPAL HOUSE FARM
118 N. River Rd., Lee, NH

As the summer begins to wane, there is no sweeter way to hold onto a little bit of its magic than with a trip to a sunflower farm, or, in this case you can make it an entire festival. The annual Sunflower Festival at Coppal House Farm along the scenic, winding roads of Lee, New Hampshire, is an event worth having on your radar, guaranteed to put a smile on your face as you drift through a cheery sea of gold and green.

Coppal House Farm began more than 3 decades ago by John and Carol Hutton, who originally purchased the 78-acre land as a dairy farm. Six sheep, two Belgian draft horses (which inspired the use of the term "coppal," or "horse" in Gaelic), three cats, a border collie, and John and Carol formed this unusual farming family. Within a relatively short time, the Huttons had not

only grown their livestock to include free-range hens and hogs and added in grain fields, but they began to host fun, community-friendly events such as corn mazes in the fall and a sunflower festival each summer.

Sunflower fields stretch over 5 acres of the farm's property, and on weekends during the festival you can find food vendors, crafts, and live music. The Coppal House Sunflower Festival spotlights oilseed sunflowers—those classic-looking sunflowers you might find at the farmers' market or your local grocer. Oilseed sunflowers have a short bloom span. The flowers at Coppal House are harvested and pressed into culinary oil sold at the farm as well as in other area local businesses. As such, the festival is a brief, but glorious happening where this beautiful flower truly gets its day in the sun.

In addition to being a fun, family-friendly event, the Coppal House Sunflower Festival is an opportunity to give back to the community. Each year the farm partners with a regional organization such as Make-A-Wish New Hampshire or CASA (Court Appointed Special Advocates) NH to donate a portion of the proceeds. What an inspired way to "grow together."

The best kind of fun in the sun.

Concord

VERRILL FARM
11 Wheeler Rd., Concord, MA

For a sunflower fix that offers more bloom varieties, head to one of Massachusetts' best-kept sunflower farm secrets: Verrill Farm in Concord. Owned and operated since 1918, the family farm has steadily grown to meet the demanding changes in the agriculture and livestock industries. Today the farm harvests an enormous array of crops from corn and pumpkins to potatoes, broccoli, radishes, and more. In addition, the farm has a large onsite market where you can purchase meat and produce grown at Verrill as well as from other locally sourced vendors.

You cannot improve upon perfection.

Verrill hosts great events during the growing season such as farm-to-table dinners and its Corn and Tomato Festival, but it's the farm's sunflower fields that steal the show.

From traditional blooms to other types like red ruby, Verrill Farm makes the most of the relatively short sunflower season. And unlike some of the busier sunflower sites, Verrill Farm is laid-back and approachable, even on the weekends when there tends to be more foot traffic in general. For a nominal ticket price, guests can take their time roaming row by row to discover the many different types of sunflowers grown at Verrill. The grounds encourage lingering and opportunities for plenty of sweet sunflower photo ops. And best of all: Each ticket price allows you to pick and cut up to five blooms to take home.

A visit to enjoy the sunflowers at Verrill is a great way to wind down summer and spend a little time marveling over how nature can create something so simple in design and yet so astonishing in its varied beauty.

A bit of Midwest charm transplanted to the Massachusetts-based Verrill Farm.

Philipston

RED APPLE FARM
455 Highland Ave., Philipston, MA

In New England a fall trip to an apple orchard is practically a law. That comes with two happy problems: 1. Which of the many orchards in the area to visit and 2. Will they have the best cider doughnuts? Fortunately, Red Apple Farms is the solution to both!

Spaulding Rose bought Red Apple Farm in 1912 from Warren Tyler, the president of Athol Savings Bank in neighboring Athol, Massachusetts. It has remained in the Rose family since, with a fourth generation of Roses steering operations and making sure the vision of the orchard as more than just a place to pick fruit, but as a way to create and sustain community, endures. They began their first harvests in 1929, and since then the family has poured its passion and hard work into making the orchard a special place to spend time and to grow many varieties of apples.

Part of Red Apple's horticultural superiority comes from its location. The farm is in the Wachusett Mountain region west of Boston, about a 20-minute drive from Wachusett Mountain itself. Situated at 1,250 feet, this makes Red Apple Farm the highest elevation orchard in New England, which translates into unique growing conditions that help produce more than 50 kinds of the most robust, flavorful apples in the region, not to mention the stunning tree-lined vistas nearly everywhere you look.

Unlike other orchards with a limited fall picking season, Red Apple is open year-round with plenty of things to do and see in just about every season. In addition to its orchards, the farm also includes pick-your-own-fruit from July through October. Stock up on farm-fresh blueberries, raspberries, peaches, and pears. In the early fall you can also visit the farm to pick corn, pumpkins, sweet squash, and even dig your own potatoes. And you can always take a break from filling your bags and treat yourself to some delicious BBQ and other tasty treats at the orchard's beautifully rustic Brew Barn. The barn is open year-round for dining and socializing whether in front of a late-fall fire or on the spacious back porch listening to outdoor music.

The Rose homestead, built in the 1700s and currently occupied by family, nestled alongside the sprawling orchard.

Throughout the year you can also find special events and happenings at the farm. Every July, Red Apple hosts a Blueberry Jamboree with specially brewed blueberry cider, blueberry glazed doughnuts, and live music. A little later on in the summer, swing back through for the Sunflower Festival, which also features live music, a fresh crop of sunny-faced sunflowers to pick, as well as stalls of local artisans and craft vendors. It's the best of what farm-fresh sustainability and time spent in nature has to offer.

And don't forget to pop into the Country Store before you leave. Inside you'll find an eclectic mixture of gift items such as tote bags, T-shirts, toys, and hand-crafted wooden serving boards along with a huge assortment of all kinds of delicious to-go goodies: locally produced jams, jellies, and syrups; spreads, dips, and seasonings; as well as candies and signature baked goods such as pies, breads, and, of course, cider doughnuts (good luck getting those home in one piece).

All of this makes Red Apple Farm sound a bit like one of those "mega-orchards" with so many offerings it can seem overwhelming—especially on a busy weekend day in October at the height of foliage and picking season. But here's the secret to what makes this orchard so special: For all its bustling fun, it maintains a homey and relaxed atmosphere. A visit to Red Apple Farm feels like spending the day at the sprawling country estate of a good friend. As you turn off the main route, a sleepy, tree-lined back road quietly crests to deliver you to the entrance of the farm. You'll want to take plenty of time meandering through the casually sprawling acreage of fruit trees that span the length of the property. Maybe you'll pause for a minute in your picking, resting underneath a towering maple, blazing with its orange crown, or leaning against one of the many massive rambling stone walls that guide visitors around the grounds. There is no shortage of places to roam and explore at your own pace. And there are lots of quiet places tucked throughout the farm just waiting for you to stop, relax, breathe in the gorgeous fall air, and, most importantly, enjoy a delicious sample (or two) of the "fruits" of your labor.

Opposite: The scenic drive to Red Apple Farm in the fall is worth the trip alone.; Sip cider or grab some food and listen to outdoor music at the Brew Barn.; Ready to pack and nibble.

Afterword

It's been an honor to get to show you a bit of the New England that has my heart and always manages to catch my eye. It's been my intention to impart some of what makes these beautiful, incredible, wholly distinct locales worth spending time getting to know. In putting this book together, I had the enormous pleasure of making my own new discoveries and finding additional parts of New England to treasure. Every destination speaks volumes. Whether you've met these places for the first time or feel inspired to give them a second look, I hope that you leave these pages energized to make your own memories, chart your own discoveries, and add your own fantastic chapter to their ongoing stories.

Acknowledgments

There are far more people whom I owe an eternal debt of gratitude to than I can name here.

My deepest thanks to Lilly Ghahremani and everyone at Full Circle Literary for the ongoing support and unflagging belief in me and my creative offerings.

Thank you to my editor, Kate Ayers, for your expert guidance, keen insights, and fantastic enthusiasm for this work. And to everyone at Globe Pequot who had a hand in bringing this project to life. Thank you to Amy Lyons for initially taking this project to the publishing team at Globe and giving me the opportunity.

Thanks to my family: Mom, Pat, Vanessa, Tim and Teddy; The Verrettes, The Longs, The Petersons; The Bentleys—for all your love and support and encouragement.

To those who have stood by me throughout this project and who have always been in my corner: Tom Pirozzoli and Kate Phelan; Willy and Cath Porter; Christina Gillease and Mary Baum; Michelle Baker; Todd Jewett; Yolanda Cellucci; David Josef and Danny Forrester; Andy Aylesworth; Bishara and Michele Shbat; Karen Harris; Janet Freed; Tracy Rosenthal-Newsom; Todd and Donna Young; Mahlon Bickford; Julie and Annette Grabowski; John Griffin; Ken Savage; Joe Krupnik; John and Michelle Bergland; Eric Pierce; Pat Furlong.

Thank you to everyone who has championed my photography, purchased calendars, and left notes and comments about how my images resonate. I am so grateful and honored.

And to Mike: I could never do this without you, and I wouldn't want to anyway.

Index

A

Arnold Arboretum 69
Ashdale Farm 173
Athol, MA 196
Auntie Kay and Uncle Frank Chin Park 58
Authors' Ridge 161

B

Back Bay 32
Bass Rocks Inn 115
Bates Hall 43
Beacon Hill 24
Beacon Hill Books & Café 31
Beauport 119
Black Cat Curiosity Shoppe 78
Bolton, MA 181, 188
Boott Cotton Mills Museum 92
Boston Harbor 58
Boston, MA 13, 14
Boston Manufacturing Company 93
Boston Public Library 38
Boston Women's Memorial 37
Brattle Book Shop 50
Brookline, MA 68

C

Cambridge, MA 49, 153, 167
Cape Ann Peninsula 104
Chandler Hovey Park 138
Charles River Esplanade 44
Charter Street Burying Point 77
Common, The 15
Commonwealth Avenue Mall 34
Concord, MA 81, 153, 154, 181
Coppal House Farm 190

Coven Cottage 78

Crane Estate, The 182

D

Damon Mill 188–89

Daniels House Inn 83

Derby Wharf Light Station 85

Dewey Square Park 58

E

Eastern Point Lighthouse 117

Eastern Point Wildlife Sanctuary 117

Edson Cemetery 100

Embrace, The 15

F

Faneuil Hall Marketplace 14

Fan Pier Park 58

Fenway Park 14

Financial District 58

Fisherman's Memorial 115

Fort Channel Park 58

Fort Sewall 137

Freedom Plaza 15

Fruitlands Farmhouse 176

Fruitlands Museum 175

G

Gloucester Harbor 115

Gloucester, MA 103, 108

Graffiti Alley 49

Great Hall 110

Great House 187

Greenway Carousel 58

Greenway, The 58

H

Halibut State Park 104

Hammond Castle Museum 109, 119

Hammond Radio Research Laboratory 110

Harvard 53

Harvard, MA 153, 175

I

Innovation District 59
Ipswich, MA 181, 182
Isabella Stewart Gardner Museum 65

J

Jack Kerouac Grave 100
Jonathan Corwin House 76

K

Kearney Square 89

L

Lapin Park 78
Lawrence, MA 93
Lee, NH 181, 190
Lexington 177
Lincoln, MA 153, 177
Louisa May Alcott's Orchard House 154
Lowell Cemetery 96
Lowell, MA 13, 88

M

Marblehead Light Station 138
Marblehead, MA 103, 134
Massachusetts Audubon Society 117
McIntire District 80
Memorial Day Flag Garden 18
Merrimack River 88
Minute Man National Historical Park 177
Minute Man Trails 178
Moffat-Ladd House 143
Mount Auburn Cemetery 167

N

Nashoba Valley Winery 188
Native American Museum 176
New Bedford, MA 69
Newburyport, MA 103, 127
North Andover, MA 153, 173
North Church 143

North End 63
North Shore Community Development Coalition 87

O

Old Manse 161
Old North Bridge 161, 177
Old North Church 63
Old Town House 136

P

Palmer Cove 85
Pawtucket Canal 88
Peirce Island 145, 148
Peirce Island Bridge 148
Pere Lachaise Cemetery 167
Pickering House 81
Plum Island, MA 103, 127
Portsmouth, NH 103, 140
Prescott Park 145, 148
Public Garden, The 19

R

Ralph Waldo Emerson House 156
Red Apple Farm 196
Rings Fountain 58
Rockport, MA 103, 104
Rocky Neck Art Colony 125
Ropes Mansion 78
Rose Fitzgerald Kennedy Greenway 53

S

Salem Common 81
Salem, MA 13, 72
Salem Maritime National Historic Site 83
Salem Witch Trials Memorial 77
Shaker Museum 176
Sleeper-McCann House 119
Sleepy Hollow Cemetery 161
South River 85
Stacy Esplanade and Fisherman's Memorial 115
Stevens-Coolidge House and Gardens 173

Strawbery Banke 144
Suffolk Mill 92

T
Tannery Marketplace 133

V
Verrill Farm 192
Visitor Center, The 92

W
Wachusett Mountain 196
Walden Pond State Reservation 158
Waltham, MA 88
Watertown, MA 167
Wedding Cake House 115
Wharf District Parks 58
World War I Memorial Bridge 148

About the Author

Sheila Moeschen is a Boston-based writer and photographer whose books include *The League of Extraordinarily Funny Women: 50 Trailblazers of Comedy*. She has a couple of fancy degrees, but her passion has always been in the creative arts. Sheila writes on humor and pop culture, and her work has appeared on The Belladonna Comedy and Medium's Fanfare pop culture publication. Her Substack publication, *Stay Curious*, is a lighter look at life and culture delivered in essays and photography with humor and heart. She is proud to call New England her lifelong home, even though she cannot tell you anything about its sports teams.